REAL ESTATE FORTUNES

NO MONEY DOWN
MILLIONAIRES
THE UNTOLD STORY

FIRST EDITION

Carlos P. and Jackie N. Reid

REID PUBLISHING

About This Book
This book is based upon the experiences of Patrick and Jackie Reid in building a real estate business. While the financial information related to their real estate investments and the real estate techniques employed by the writers are true and actually happened, the stories in the book are intended merely to illustrate the writers' experiences and are not intended to refer to actual persons, whether living or dead. Some of the characters in the book are composites. To provide foundation and texture to the book's narrative structure, some parts of the book are based on information from third parties. In lieu of using terminology such as "Jane or John Doe" or "Subject Property 1 or 15", all character names, as well as the names of the properties and locations described in the book, have been made up by the writers. This book should be considered an expression of the writers' observations and opinions with regard to the characters and events depicted in the book, and not as a representation of actual fact as to any particular individual or event:

REAL ESTATE FORTUNES: NO MONEY DOWN MILLIONAIRES; THE UNTOLD STORY

Copyright@ 2008 by Carlos and Jackie Reid

Cover art copyright @ 2008 Carlos and Jackie Reid

Library of Congress Control Number: xxxxxxxxxxx

ISBN-13: 978-0-6152-4264-4
ISBN-10: x-xxx-xxxxx-x

Manufactured in the United States of America

Dedication

This one is for our parents Bill and Patricia Reid and George and Betty Neville.

Author's Acknowledgments

Special thanks are necessary to Kathy Neville whose guidance, wisdom, and encouragement made this work possible. Thanks to all our "Angel Tenants" (and you know who you are), Eugene Williams, George and the late Celia Hill for making all the hardships easier and sometimes comical. We also would like to thank Woody, Jerry, Donni, Lisa, Gina, Bonnie, John and Lu who listened to our stories and gave encouragement even through the most nauseating events. Diane Alire, thank you for the excellent book cover.

CONTENTS

CONTENTS

CONTENTS

Introduction

If Even *I* Can Do It...

It's 2am and I'm sitting in front of my new 52-inch plasma TV. It's mounted on the wall of our beachfront condo, Pensacola Beach. I look out the sliding hurricane-glass door to my left and see that the full moon has illuminated the Gulf to a vivid emerald green. The gentle waves stir up a glowing white froth that rolls softly up the sugar-like sand. I'm wearing the classic attire for an early morning Frig run – a pair of Hanes tighty whities – as I sit Indian style on our L-shaped wrap around couch. Polishing off my second bowl of Cheerios, I've managed to splash only a little milk on the floor and couch as I resituate my posture and slug the remnants down.

I can't sleep. For whatever reason, I'm nervous and need some reassurance. So I click though the TV channels until I come to that ubiquitous 2am infomercial: the seemingly endless train of talking heads rave about No Money Down...cashflow...the genuine beauty of real estate millions. The same couples we've all seen a dozen times before flash on the TV screen. All of them discuss their success in real estate. The minister. The cute black couple. The farmer who'd lost his home in a fire. The young couple with no education. The same people every time.

I tell this story because these people from the infomercial – these No Money Down Real Estate Millionaires – are all my brothers and sisters. Figuratively, of course. We share the same journey, you see. I smile as I watch Carlton with his "magic sheets." I nod along with another baldheaded guy touting a cashflow plan. I recognize an approach eerily similar to the book *Rich Dad, Poor Dad*. I watch with rapt attention as another young guy with too much product in his hair talks about foreclosures.

Obviously, if you've seen any of these commercials, you recall that many of them are filmed in a Hawaii-type setting. Sunshine and palm trees and smiling faces are everywhere. It's effective, this technique. And while the shots of paradise might inspire most people looking to make their riches, they tend to bring me peace. Maybe that's because I've already made mine – and amassed my relative wealth doing exactly as these infomercial actors claim to have done themselves. They calm me, these testimonials. And after awhile, my eyelids begin to sag. Sleep has come, finally. So I return to bed and snuggle up to my wife, Jackie. Under the covers, my hand finds her tiny hand and I fall asleep.

We've been together for over 27 years, Jackie and I. Still just in our early 40's, we now enjoy a semi-retired lifestyle in Pensacola Beach, Florida. But we've made our way – so why, then, would we take the time to write a book? The idea stemmed from these infomercials I've just discussed. We were drawn by them, too. We bought in to the idea. And you know what? It *worked* for us, but not without a whole lot of roadblocks and setbacks along the way.

And besides, we've managed to build up a nice laidback lifestyle for ourselves. Whenever we talk about being semi-retired, we get so many different responses from the people we meet. They range from "lucky" to "son of a bitch" to "how in the world could you be semi-retired already?" Regardless of the response, we tell anyone who wants to know that we own commercial real estate; that we rent out apartments and duplexes; that we've renovated and flipped homes. When we reveal this little fact, there's usually only one response: "Oh. That makes perfect sense!"

Like us, most people who respond in this way have seen the 2am *No Money Down Real Estate* infomercials. All morning long, it is one testimonial after another; millionaire after millionaire living on the beach as they harvest equity and cash from their real estate holdings. No further response or explanation is typically required. Everyone gets it. But why then, do so few actually attempt it?

The main reason that we write this book is to show a different side to the No Money Down story. Make no mistake, No Money Down *is* effective. It *does* work. And it works extremely well. But if you're going to jump into the real estate game – if you envision yourself renting dozens of properties out to promptly paying, harmonious tenants – then you need a sincere wakeup call. If you have tried the real estate game already and have met with less success than you anticipated, you are likely to find solace in many of these stories. Regardless of your experience, what you will find in the pages to come is a clear and honest picture of what it takes to make a fortune with No Money Down.

Please don't misunderstand our intentions. We firmly believe that these systems work. We are living proof that they do work, in fact. But if you hope to make your millions on one of them, you have to understand that the term "blood, sweat, and tears" applies here. Actually, "blood, sweat, and tears" doesn't necessarily cover it all. As you'll see, cashflow systems designed for financial independence or getting rich quick involve much more. Maybe we should invent a new term for it: "blood, sweat, tears, murder, drugs, disappointment, courage, crooks, and...angels."

Getting Started

Our adventure began in 1983, soon after Jackie and I married. I had accepted an ROTC scholarship from the Army, which helped me pay for my final two years of college. I would go on to earn a degree in Geology from the University of Alabama while Jackie worked at the famous Bo jangles Fried Chicken. Following my graduation, I was shipped off to my European tour of duty and stationed in Mannheim, Germany for four years. Jackie came along and stayed on the base. I received an honorable discharge from the Army in 1988, so the two of us could then return to civilian life in Alabama.

Being young and naïve, I was naturally excited about the possibility of being able to finally start my career as a Geologist. But I quickly learned at job interviews that my degree was severely aged. I was told that I would need to go back to graduate school if I hoped to get any of the jobs I'd been dreaming of. Only problem was that I was broke.

So Jackie and I moved to an area in west-central Alabama, where I got a job at a chemical waste plant in Louisville. Only the highest level of work for me at the plant – I did something akin to performing fingerprint analysis on the waste in order to verify that it was indeed waste and worthy of disposal (God only knows what was in my system from working at that place). It was around the time that I started pulling the swing shift that I realized it just wasn't worth it to remain there. Jackie hated when I worked the night shift because she was always determined to stay up all night so she would be tired enough to sleep next to me when I got home in the morning. It took its toll on both of us. We were exhausted all the time.

So it was time for a change and the real estate business came calling. I signed up for the Alabama Real Estate course and soon received a license to sell. At the time, I think my self-esteem was a little too low to be a good agent. I mean, I'd never even lived in a real home before, so I felt extremely out of place when showing clients these giant and beautiful houses. See, I grew up in the back addition of a motel in Butler, Alabama, a place owned and operated by my parents. I had a great childhood. Three brothers. But I think my low self-esteem maybe came from the fact that I basically grew up in the life of a servant.

Dad ran a good business. He made his money. But I remember things from my childhood like running down the sidewalks with towels and ice buckets, frantic to deliver these items to waiting guests. I would run and jump barefooted into the rooms. It's funny to think about now, but my greatest fear as a child was upsetting the guests so much that they wouldn't like their stay and would never come back. It wasn't until much later that I realized we had only three kinds of guests: people working at the nearby mill, people who had gotten lost on the road, and people who were looking for a room for a quick lay. No, regardless of how hard we all worked, none of them would ever be coming back.

It was the 70s. The days of disco fever and Earth, Wind, and Fire. Afros and silk shirts and those incredibly tall shoes. My dad knew all the players, who in turn loved my dad because he could provide them and their lady friends with a room for an hour or two (and sometimes, for as little as five minutes). You've heard the phrase "No tell Motel." My dad practically invented it! My brother Charlie and I were of course left to change the sheets and rinse out the sinks afterwards. You can imagine.

Don't get me wrong, though. I had a good childhood by most standards. My parents were strong and loving and possessed of honest character.

Why am I telling you these stories? Well, first off, I just wanted you to know all the things that motivated me to work toward a better life. But more importantly, I wanted to demonstrate that *anyone* – even a naïve young man with a servant's upbringing, a military background, and a relatively useless degree – can make it in this business if they're willing to put in the legwork.

But I digress. In my determination not to end up working the swing shift at the Paper mill, I managed to sell only one home during my real estate career. It was a nice turn of luck for Jackie and me because the interest rate at the time was 11-14 percent!

No, I wasn't terribly successful at traditional real estate selling. But it did teach me many important things, the most important coming from a Century 21 creative financing course. The course was well over my head, as you can imagine, but I did get to the point where I could better understand the minds of bankers – how they think and what they want, why they like the down payment, what percentages they use to calculate the affordability of a property, and how they employ loan to value ratios.

With this information, I learned that I could buy a house *without* a down payment. And it was right there that the beast was born.

My career as a real estate salesman lasted about six months before I landed a good job as a conservation officer with the State of Alabama. Being a conservation officer was the most fun I ever had – sneaking around property, looking for poachers, high speed chases, gunfights, robotic deer, and working with a cast of characters that would fill an entire novel. This job, although trying at times, also featured flexible hours. To be a successful game warden, I would work from 6am to 10am. Then, I'd take a break and return to work from 3pm to 6pm. Obviously, this schedule gave me five hours in the middle of the day to work on other projects...but what could I possibly work on?

The Initial Investment – Our First Home

Jackie and I were living in a tiny two-bedroom apartment on Highway 110 in Hasselville, Alabama. Jackie was working as the bookkeeper with the local newspaper, which was nice because it afforded her insight into the houses coming on the market. In short order, she uncovered a lead on a small three-bedroom, one-bathroom house on South Cedar Street (a great, centrally located neighborhood). The house was for sale by owner and had been on the market for more than six months. The owners had already moved away, and so were pretty desperate to sell. The asking price was a meager $38,000.

We loved the place immediately, and it was priced right. Plus, I was eager to put to the test the knowledge I'd recently gleaned from my short real estate career. I wanted to see if I could purchase this house with no money down. So during my next break from work, I went to the courthouse and located the deed and the mortgage. The document revealed the date the owners had purchased the home, the loan amount, and the fact that the loan carried a fifteen-year term.

The mortgage documents didn't show the interest rate, but I asked around and learned that at the time of purchase, rates were around 11 percent. Using an amortization schedule, I calculated that the current owners still owed the bank $33,000. So that's the amount I offered. They countered at $35,000, which was as low as they would go. ($33,000 plus $2000 real estate commission.)So I took the deal.

My next step was to go to the bank and have them run an appraisal. They came back with a nice little figure: $42,000. This was nice for a couple of reasons. First, it meant that my home was already worth way more than I paid for it. Second, the price I'd negotiated relative to the market price of the home eliminated the need for a down payment (initially, the bank would only cover 80 percent of the market value, preferring that I put 20 percent down, but since my purchase price amounted to only 78 percent of the total market value of the home, I could just take out the loan without making the down payment). Full disclosure: I did wind up making a $500 token payment – just to keep the suits happy – but the bottom line is that I walked out of there with my first home.

We would live in this house for several years, Jackie and I, but on that first day, we learned that we'd have our work cut out for us in the near term. Its value may have been $42,000, but it had clearly been neglected by renters. Still, after a coat of paint and few touchups, I was confident that we could get over $40,000 for the property. So we had between $5,000 and $7,000 of equity in our first home. Not bad.

Expansion into Rental Houses

Sufficiently sold on the value of real estate buying, I began looking for potential rental properties. Luckily, in a conversation with our accountant, Betty Sue, I came upon what seemed like an excellent opportunity. Betty Sue was preparing our income tax returns, as she had done the previous year. Being a businesswoman who owned a trailer park herself, she was no stranger to the money that could be made and the benefits that could be accrued in acquiring rental property. Anyway, she put me in touch with a contact of hers named Vernon Smith, who informed us that he had been trying to sell a duplex he owned for some time.

When I called, I found a man very eager to sell a duplex. Coincidentally, the price for this place was also set at $38,000. Smith claimed that it would reap an income of $500 per month. That seemed like a pretty sweet deal –

maybe a little too sweet – so I calculated the mortgage, taxes, and insurance and came to the conclusion that we could only expect to clear $100 per unit, per month (or $200 total).

Still, it seemed like a reasonable opportunity to enter the rental game. And being as naïve as I was at the time, it sounded to me like free money, this $200 per month. So I picked up a newspaper and showed the duplex to Jackie. Together, we inspected the property and determined that it was in good shape (it had a new roof and flooring, after all). The tenants seemed favorable, as the Smiths had previously lived in one of the units while Bob Johnson, Vernon's stepson, was living in the other. We were also delighted to find that the vacant unit had already been rented out to the McInnis family, as well.

Jackie liked the duplex, but more importantly, she liked how excited I sounded about buying it. "Let's just go for it," she said. "And I'll do whatever I can to help."

With my wife's stamp of approval, I went enthusiastically to the courthouse and pulled up the mortgage. Again, my calculations found a much lower number than the asking price. Smith still owed the bank $27,000, so I offered $30,000. He countered at $33,000, which is where we closed the deal.

Now we owned a home with $5,000 equity and our first rental property with $200 excess income which I reckoned was around $20,000.00 additional equity. These two transactions increased our net worth $25,000 in just three months!

Properly energized by that thought, I continued the search to acquire more property.

We bought a small house on Marvin Street for $21,000, and rented it out for $350.00 per month. Another $100 a month in the bank. We stumbled across an estate house on Depot Street, and we purchased it for $15,000, renting it out for $300 per month. Another $200 per month in the bank. A duplex and a house on Jefferson street were going for a package deal at $25,000. After renting out all we could, it was another $300 per month in the bank.

Things just snowballed from there. Five duplexes were put up for sale at once – half a city block for $99,000. The rental income easily justified the price. The units were in fairly poor condition (falling ceiling tiles, leaks under most of the bathtubs, siding worn off, and termite damage), but Jackie and I talked it over and decided that we should just do it. Jackie even bought me a Nike t-shirt with those words on it. We made a $90,000 offer and settled at $95,000. The bank was kind enough to finance it no money down.

So after all this activity, we had finally established ourselves as commercial real estates investors. We were clearing around $1800 per month on all our properties. We owned so many units that we were already starting to develop a reputation for being landlords in the area. I won't get into the meat and potatoes of the labor that went along with it at this point – the rest of the book will provide plenty of horror stories – but suffice to say that it wasn't all buy and sell to get to this point. It was hard work. Extremely hard work. I found myself spending long hours each day making essential repairs and renovating units as they became vacant...and then there were the tenants...

No Money Down *Works*

The months and years that would follow would bring a great deal of excitement, trial and error, and ultimately riches for my wife and me. Our transactions would begin to drift well into the six figure range, and every time we would complete one, our net worth would swell considerably. By the time we began looking into our first large rental property – a 24-unit complex called Carriage Hill Apartments – things were looking very promising indeed.

I remember the day I realized that Jackie and I had turned the corner on this no money down formula. While qualifying for the loan on Carriage Hill, I began to see the effect of the income properties on our credit application. The incomes were taken at face value, so qualifying for loans became easier and easier with each fresh purchase we made. At the time, I was dumb enough to think that the bank was wrong to assume such a high value for our property investments. Looking back now, I can see what the mortgage underwriters knew: that regardless of my competence as a real estate owner, these holdings were appreciating at a rapid rate.

Our business had grown. Between our apartments and single family homes, we had over eighty residences to our name. Jackie quit her job at the newspaper. A year later, I resigned from my State job and we worked together full time on our real estate. Years later, we would sell the Carriage Hill complex and move to Pensacola Beach. These days, we travel to Hasselville on Mondays to pick up rent checks and pay our property manager.

I tell you what: it was terrifying leaving the security of that State job. I have this recurring nightmare where I've forgotten to turn in my weekly reports to my supervisor. Sometimes, the nightmare concerns a strong desire to get my old job back. By the time I realize that I've already turned in my guns, uniforms, and vehicles, I've woken up in a cold sweat. From there, I usually wander into the kitchen to grab a bowl of Cheerios and watch my friends on the real estate infomercials.

It wasn't easy getting to where I am today. And that's why Jackie and I sit down now to write this book. You've seen the No Money Down commercials and you've read the many books on the subject. What you're going to get here is the underbelly of the process. What these pages will show you is that buying and renting out homes isn't always sunshine and roses and living in Hawaii. You have to get your hands dirty. You have to deal with headache tenants. You'll break your back with labor (both the physical side and the financial side of labor). You will make your millions, yes, but you'll also have to be willing to *earn* them.

Read on to discover all the growing pains Jackie and I had to endure as real estate buyers and landlords. You will read stories that will inspire you. You will read stories that might give you pause. You will read stories that are downright bizarre and stories that are entirely gross. But in the end you will learn all the things that I didn't know when I first got into the real estate business – and they are sure to help you greatly as you move forward.

But before I close this introduction, I'd just like to say one thing. As I sit here in my beach house, typing in my underwear, there's one thought that brings a smile to my face: though I may have made some mistakes along the way, though I may have pursued a lifestyle that not everyone has the stomach or the heart for, if I could go back and do it all again, I wouldn't change a thing.

Chapter One

Low Income Tenants

Again, it's not my intention to talk you out of pursuing the *No Money Down* Real Estate path. If it's something that interests you, please do pursue it. But before I can get in to the nuts and bolts of the kinds (and the sheer level) of work you should expect to be doing, I'm going to hit you with a few horror stories. See, dealing with tenants of any kind is difficult. You'll get people who can't pay or refuse to pay. You'll get people who destroy things that don't belong to them. You'll get people who treat the place like a giant litter box. It's not pretty. And it's not easy.

We'll begin with low income tenants because that's where I started my millionaire landlord career – and that's most likely where you'll kick off yours. As I said, tenants of any kind and of any income can be trouble at times, but low income tenants, as a general rule, tend to be hell.

I know this No Money Down stuff all sounds pretty simple and neat, but you're now going to get the details on the properties and the characters Jackie and I had to learn to manage (and learn to manage the hard way).

The general **Lesson #1**, as Jackie and I saw it: it helps to play good cop, bad cop when approaching the different situations that arise when dealing with the kinds of environments and personalities you'll encounter in renting out properties. In our little arrangement, Jackie was usually the good cop. She was better at it. But, man, if you ever crossed the good cop...

Alright, let's get this party started with stories from one of our very first duplexes. Davis 701A and 701B is a duplex with two 3 bedroom/1 bathroom apartments. I say "is" because we still own this property and have lately managed to maintain steady renters. Today, it brings in a rental income of $690.00 per month. We don't owe anything on the property, so it produces a nice income for us.

But that wasn't always the case...

The Demolition Woman

When we'd first bought the Davis duplex, we were happy to have inherited some nice tenants in 701A. The McInnis family always paid their rent on time. But unfortunately, as these things go, they moved out a few years after we bought he place. So we had to get 701A ready to rent again. I'll get into all the gory details of renovating in Chapter 5, but right now, it's enough to say that we'd just finished dressing this place up and setting out the For Rent sign when a short, chubby woman approached Jackie, who was loading up the truck.

"That apartment available?" she asked.

Jackie nodded.

"Well my name is Ms. Tallie and I'd like to rent it."

We were thrilled. We couldn't imagine an easier transition process. *Maybe this renting thing will be easier than I thought,* I remember thinking. Jackie started the application process and discovered that Ms. Tallie was gainfully employed and had enough income to pay the

$250.00 a month we were asking. As she had several children, the Tallie family was in desperate need of a place to live. She paid the deposit and first month's rent and moved in the following Saturday. What a dream she seemed to be.

I remember that the power and water hadn't been switched on yet – they just moved in so quickly – and the family Tallie would have to wait until Monday for it to be running again. Jackie (always the good cop) felt bad for the kids, so she took Ms. Tallie a cooler of ice filled with drinks and some snacks for them to enjoy. When I think now about what that woman would put us through, I'm not sure I'd have let Jackie leave the house with that much free stuff.

Even from the beginning, Ms. Tallie seemed like a nice lady. She worked long hours and was always fawning over her kids. For several months, our new tenant paid her rent on time (she had little choice, as Jackie would go by her place of employment to collect). But that quickly came to a halt when she took another job at a place owned and operated by "the Bishop."

Now a little background on the Bishop (or "the Deacon," to some): He ran a kind of cultish organization. He owned motels and gas stations, and all of his employees were members of his cult. These people worked hard in exchange for the right to live in the Bishop's compound. Unlike most of his employees, Ms. Tallie was not a part of the cult, so she was just on the payroll – which apparently didn't afford her enough cash to cover her rent as well as the upkeep of the apartment.

Tenant behind on rent? That's when bad cop comes calling. I went over to 701A and knocked loudly on the door.

Ms. Tallie barely opened the door. She peaked her head through the small crack. Readers, I can't stress this enough: if a tenant opens a door like this, they obviously don't want you to see what's inside. No dummy, I pushed the door open wider and told her that I needed to talk to her about the rent. Let me tell you, I was *shocked* at what I saw when I stepped inside. I rubbed my eyes in disbelief. It just didn't seem possible that someone could do so much damage to a place, for one thing, but also actually continue to live in that place, for another.

And this was my investment that we're talking about here. It was in shambles. Still, I dared to inspect the place.

First, I went into the bathroom, where I gagged immediately, realizing that the water had been turned off and the family had continued to use the toilet as if it was still a working toilet. When that apparently got to be too much, Ms. Tallie's family had obviously turned to pissing and shitting in a five-gallon bucket and then stepping into the tub and dumping the feces out the bathtub window. When I went outside, I found that shit and piss were running down the back wall of the house. I turned around to see Ms. Tallie standing behind me. Her stare was completely blank.

"Why are you so upset?" she asked.

I shook my head in disbelief, saying nothing as I went back inside and continued walking from room to room, feeling more and more disgusted and ashamed with each stop.

The damage was devastating. There was a large hole in every last wall of sheetrock. Every doorknob and hinge was broken. None of the light fixtures or flooring outlets were working. The ceiling fans and lights were all hanging from the wires. It was as if I had hired this family to come in and start demolition for renovation. Everything that could be touched was broken.

When I came to her bedroom door, I found a padlock on it. "Unlock it," I said to her.

She slowly did as I asked. "I just wanted to protect my stuff, you know?" she said. "Don't want the kids stealing all my money."

I glanced inside the bedroom and immediately shut the door. You don't want to know.

Back in the living room, I told Ms. Tallie that she had to move out. She started crying and begging me to let her stay. She begged all the way out to the driveway, where I repeated that she had to go, cranked up my truck, and backed out. Never in my wildest imaginings would I have guessed that people could or would choose to live in this condition. I ran through in my head the items I'd need to renovate the place. By the time I got to my own driveway, the renovation costs had climbed well into the thousands.

Jackie met me at the door because she'd just gotten off the telephone with Ms. Tallie. Not knowing the condition of the apartment, my wife asked if there was any way we could let the Demolition Woman stay. "She said she'd have the rent money and the utilities she owes," she said.

I didn't know what to do because the expenses, mortgage, and the vacant adjacent apartment kept running through my mind. "When will she have the money?" I asked.

"Later today." Jackie rubbed her hand on my chest, looking at me with dewy eyes. "She was crying so much, Patrick. Begging. I just couldn't tell her no."

We decided that even though the conditions were horrendous, we could maybe teach her to clean and turn the place around while she continued to pay rent. So we slept on it before making the final decision to collect the money she owed and let her stay in the apartment.

Well, fortunately for us, we learned very quickly (and fairly painlessly) that you don't give a tenant like this a second chance. The next morning, the police called to let Jackie and I know that they had to kick in the front door to 701A so they could arrest Ms. Tallie's son for selling drugs. I thanked them and assured them that we'd have fresh tenants just as soon as the legal system helped us kick things into gear. That afternoon, we filed the eviction papers.

The Freeloaders

Let's turn now to 701B, because man, that was no picnic, either. This will be a long section. I think 701B is cursed.

I mentioned inheriting the McInnis family. Well, when we first bought the Davis duplex, we also inherited another tenant in 701B: Bob Johnson. Don't let the neutral name fool you; this guy was the stepson of the previous duplex owner; and this guy was a first class prick. And he would start a long chain of tenants that were little more than freeloaders just looking for a place to crash until the rent got too backed up to stay.

Anyway, Bob Johnson. Since we bought the property mid-month, we had in our contract a stipulation that Jackie and I were to receive all prorated rent. Bob didn't pay. So I went over and knocked on the door. Introduced myself. Asked for the rent.

"I gave it to Vernon," he told me gruffly.

I nodded and thanked him. Later, I called Vernon, who informed me that his attorney had advised him that he didn't have to pay me the rent because he had collected it before we completed the closing. I remained calm and said that it was clear in our agreement that he was supposed to provide the prorated rent. He told me he didn't think so and hung up.

So Jackie and I decided to go back to see Bob, who is about 6'2" and weighs around 200 pounds. At the time, Bob was drawing workmen's compensation and seeking disability. I'll have a bunch more on tenants with disability later in the chapter, but for now it just bears mentioning. Of course, I was familiar with Bob already because as a game warden I would see him fishing at the river. Considering that he was on disability, I was astonished at how fast he could load and unload his big bass boat and could stand in one place and fish for hours.

Jackie stayed in the car while I knocked on the front door. Bob merely cracked the door, so I pushed it open so that he would have to make eye contact with me. I told him he owed me the rent for this unit and that he would pay it or get out. I told him that I didn't care what kind of shady deal or scam he thought he and Vernon were going to pull on me this month, but that I owned the property and he was going to pay the rent. I was so furious that I was shaking when I walked back to the car. Jackie looked at me and asked if I got the rent.

"Shit," I said, looking squarely at my wife. "What were we thinking, getting in to this rental business?"

That same day, Vernon actually called and agreed to pay the rent – even though he ignorantly claimed that he was just doing me a favor. I collected the $200 from him later in the afternoon. $200 might not seem like much, but you have to understand that it was our money for the mortgage.

Of course, I found out later that Bob never paid Vernon the rent he claimed to have paid. Bob was lazy and probably never paid Vernon a dime of rent the whole time he lived there. In fact, now that I think about it, Bob was probably the reason Vernon sold that property in the first place – he just wanted to unload the freeloader. Incidentally, under our watch, Bob only stuck around for another 90 days or so. I guess he just got tired of living there after the free ride was taken away from him.

Freeloading Tenants Lesson #1, reader: Never rent out to your family. (Unless it's me...ha...ha ...Betty...ha?).

701B was vacant for a week after the first freeloader moved out. I was just starting to work on repairs to the unit when a very sweet lady named Virginia Lawson approached me, looking for an apartment for her daughter, Billie Jean. Virginia had worked hard all her life and had retired from a job with a telecom company in Detroit. Billie Jean looked nice – maybe a little slow – and she seemed fine. She didn't make enough money to afford the $250 rent on her own, but Virginia said that she would make sure the rent was paid.

I decided to rent her the apartment and so we signed the lease. As we all stood inside the place, looking around, Virginia pointed toward the back porch and told me she needed to tell me something.

Outside, Virginia got right down to brass tacks: "Billie will lie in a minute, so watch her and don't let her get one over on you."

I was shocked to hear such blunt words coming from the mouth of a mother. "What did you say?" I asked in disbelief.

She quickly said that Billie could be careless about paying the rent and that she might lie about how her money is being spent. I agreed to keep an eye out, but only on the condition that Virginia be added to the lease herself. She agreed and even gave me a telephone number. Feeling a little better about things, I handed Billie Jean the keys.

Freeloading Tenants Lesson #2: If the mother doesn't trust your tenant, how the hell can *you* trust your tenant?

Well, as I'll reveal in Chapter 2, Billie Jean wasn't necessarily the problem. Neither was collecting rent – we had the doting Virginia for that. Call this a brief prelude to the lessons in Chapter 2, but Billie Jean let her boyfriend move in (and he was never put on the lease) and all hell broke loose. Long story short, Billie Jean and her freeloading boyfriend had to go.

We had a few other tenants between Billie Jean and the man who would be our latest freeloader, but we'll cover those in later chapters, as their stories apply well to the ideas that 1) collecting rent sometimes sucks and 2) allowing a spouse or significant other to move in without signing a lease is always a bad idea. For now, let's talk about Travis Benson, the next in our long line of cheapskates and hustlers.

Travis filled out an application and said he worked at Rights Company, an established firm in Hasselville. I met the son of the man who owned the company (Tim Right was the son's name) and he claimed to be very pleased with Travis' work ethic and accountability.

Freeloading Tenants Lesson #3: All prospective tenants claim to be trustworthy; always call their employer to get a second opinion.

In this case, Lesson #3 made me feel all warm inside – Tim Right gave me a glowing recommendation – but even it would prove to be less than foolproof in the end. But I decided to rent the apartment to Travis.

Jackie was pumped when I called her, because it was starting to seem to both of us like we'd never get a winner in 701B. "Let's get some beer and grill out tonight," she said. "You know…celebrate."

I agreed. And we had fun. But the fun would soon slow...

Travis paid his rent for the first two months. No problem. But when he didn't pay the third month, I had to go in to Rights Company to talk to him. I asked one of the men who worked there if I could speak with Travis. The guy looked at me and said, "Oh, Travis? He got fired because he's been stealing from us for years." Apparently, they'd caught the deadbeat taking money out of the register, then going to the back and dropping it out the door for Ms. Patsy Benson to pick up."

So let's add an addendum to Lesson #3: Sometimes even second opinions need second opinions; consider the source of your referral before you believe in its credibility.

I wanted to punch Tim Right in the face because he had given me such a great recommendation for Travis. But I remained calm and returned to the unit. When I stepped inside, I was surprised to find an older woman with bad hair sitting in a chair, smoking a cigarette. And when I say "old," I mean *old*. She looked like she might be in her hundreds. She was Ms. Patsy, I discovered – Travis's mother.

"I'll take care of the rent," she told me. She even gave me her personal phone number.

Yeah.

For a couple of months, Jackie would call Ms. Patsy to let her know that we would be coming by to collect the rent. By this time, there were ten to twelve people living in this place. Picture that. A three bedroom place. Ten to twelve people. Most of them grown men playing cards and drinking beer all day.

Picture this, too: Me exiting our car in the driveway of Ms. Patsy's house which was only two blocks away from 701B; Jackie climbing into the driver's seat (you know, just in case we would need to tear out of there if the ten to twelve card players got a little physical); and me knocking on the door, not taking any guff from the drunks, and asking to see the matron of the house. Inevitably, someone would stumble to the back of the house, where they would fetch Ms. Patsy, who would waddle up and fork over the money. I'd graciously accept and hand her a receipt in return. She'd look proud. There she was, the powerful matriarch running a group home without permission.

All the freeloaders under Ms. Patsy's care (and under Travis' original lease), received some form of welfare check. From what I understand, they would hand Patsy their check and she would pool it all together and pay the rent. She'd even pay for their smokes and alcohol. I would later find out that, for spending cash, these people would roam around stealing or shoplifting. Ms. Patsy's address was well known to the police and was always listed in the police arrest report. Not a good thing for us, as you can imagine.

Well, this relationship finally ended when I decided to run a routine maintenance check on 701B. I found the usual crowd there, of course, but I also found something I wasn't expecting: the faucet to the kitchen sink had been broken off and water was flowing freely onto the kitchen floor. I asked why no one had reported this problem to Jackie or me and was met with blank stares. Imagine their water bill. It must have skyrocketed. I guess Patsy had plenty of cash to cover the bill. Otherwise, we'd have gotten a call immediately.

But that's just the point, reader. Sometimes, a tenant will just let your place go to hell. The only time they care about damage is if it directly affects *them*.

I called Ms. Patsy immediately. "Get these people out of the apartment or I'm evicting them," I said.

She paused, waffling.

"Alright, then," I said quickly. "Get them out today and you'll get your full deposit refunded."

I guess she needed more cash than I gave her credit for, because the rabble of freeloaders was out by the end of the day.

The Dealers

Shortly after the purchase of the Davis duplex and during the 701A/B episodes, Jackie and I purchased a 2-bedroom house on Marvin Street. This place was in a strange little crossroads area called Springfield – and I say "strange" because the neighborhood was cut right down the middle of the aesthetic picture: half the houses being absolute shacks and the other half being small but legitimately homey looking places. No matter. I liked the area because it was near three different industrial plants and within walking distance to a beautifully managed Federal park and RV site flush with baths and boat landings. Potential for tenants galore.

Not surprisingly, the first two tenants at Marvin Street were a Federal Park Ranger and, later, a State of Alabama biologist. Sounds like a pair of good tenants, right? Well, reader, they were. They were dream tenants, in fact. Seemed at the time like Jackie and I were finally catching a break.

Anyway, the Ranger and the Biologist confessed to liking the house because it was cheap and it was one of the few places that allowed pets. For two years, the Marvin house was great. With our excellent two tenants always promptly dropping off the rent, the house was paying for itself. For the first time, Jackie and I began to think that owning real estate was in fact a viable way to be your own boss and make money.

But as they say, all good things must come to an end – and the little honeymoon period with the Marvin house was no different.

The Biologist was the first to pack up and move. He had become a good friend of ours over the two years he lived there, and so he came to me in search of advice on the purchase of his own home. That was a bittersweet for me: On the one hand, I was bitter because I knew it meant I'd be losing one of my only good tenants; on the other, it was pretty sweet to know that somebody thought of me as an expert on *something*.

So I gave him advice – good advice, unfortunately, as it would lead to the quick purchase of a new home for the Biologist. Jackie and I hated to see him move, but at the same time, we were happy with his excitement to finally start living the American Dream of homeownership. Plus, he left us with very few repairs to deal with – a coat of paint and a little wipe down and we were ready for the next tenant.

Another trustworthy Biologist please? Nope. I guess maintaining our sanity just wasn't meant to be. Instead of calm and reliable, we got a long string of deadbeats who couldn't pay.

The next tenant was an unmarried couple from our hometown. They eventually got behind on the rent, so we had to ask them to move out.

The tenant that followed was a tall good-looking guy named Sam. He, his wife Eva, and their two beautiful children seemed like the picture of healthy American living. They immediately liked the house – and they even had the proper cash it would take to move in.

"What do you do for a living?" I remember asking him as we stood outside, having just finished the preliminary tour of the Marvin house.

"I cut hair down at ABC House of Styles," I remember him saying. "Eva doesn't work."

Warning bells should have flashed for me, but they didn't. I just smiled and handed over the keys.

Dealers Lesson #1: If you have a family of four and only one person works (and he/she likely makes minimum wage), one of two things is true: either A) you've got a tenant who will quickly fall behind on rent or B) you've got a tenant who gets his/her money the wrong way...

What did we do, Jackie and I? We approved the application and they moved in. After we closed the deal, Jackie and I drove to Meridian, Mississippi to see a movie, have dinner, and make our usual stop at Lowe's for a maintenance supply list. We talked about how nice the couple seemed to be and how cute the kids were. Jackie was glad to know that the kids would be able to enjoy the nice yard and nearby park at Marvin house.

A couple months later, we rode by the house on our way to the park and noticed that our new tenants had a pit bull caged up in a pen they'd built in the back yard. **Dealers Lesson #2**: Drug dealers like pit bulls.

At the time, we thought little of it. Just a pet for the kids to enjoy. And who were we to judge if they had chosen such a notoriously aggressive dog? Besides, they were paying their rent on time, so what did we care? Long story short, by the middle of the third month, Jackie and I started getting complaints from the neighbors. First, the complaints were about the dog and its barking. But later, Jackie started receiving calls from concerned neighbors who claimed that the people in our house were drug dealers.

Our first reaction was to laugh it off. That picturesque family? There was no way. But then, the calls just kept coming. So I called the police in search of information on the couple – and just as had been the case during the application process, the police had no records of criminal or civil activity for the family.

So we laughed it off again, deciding that the calls from the neighbors must have been racially motivated (see, this picturesque new family was black). The closest neighbor to the Marvin house seemed to be particularly charged up – and definitely confirmed our suspicions about racial motives by almost constantly streaming the "N" word during his increasingly frequent calls.

I'd just keep telling this neighbor the same thing I always told him: that I'd called the cops already and that nothing had turned up. "Why don't you call the sheriff's department yourself?" I remember asking one time.

"That son of a bitch next door is the head dealer," he spouted. "And you know what? The cops are in on it, too. They're dirty!"

Well that about did it. We stopped taking these calls seriously. Talk about paranoid. **Dealer Lesson #3**: Paranoia is a good thing. When it comes to sniffing out dealers, it's best to err on the side of caution.

One night Jackie answered the telephone and a man asked if she was the owner of the house on Marvin Street.

"Yes, sir," she said.

"That house might burn to the ground," was the reply. Then, the caller hung up.

Not a woman to be trifled with, Jackie dialed "Star-69" and got the caller's number. She then called information and gave the operator the number in exchange for the caller's name and address. It belonged to Mr. Tucker, one of the more vocal of the "concerned neighbors" on Marvin Street. Jackie called the number and asked if she could speak to Mr. Tucker.

"This is him," he said.

"Mr. Tucker," my wife replied, "this is Jackie Reid and you just called me and threatened that my house may burn."

Needless to say, Tucker, the idiot, was shocked. "How'd you get my number?" he pleaded, confounded. "Now if something happens to that house, you're going to think that I did it."

Jackie just sighed. "You're the one that said it, Mr. Tucker, not me. Let's just hope it doesn't burn."

A day or two later, Jackie went by Marvin house to collect the rent, but found no one at home. It being the due date, she decided to call ABC House of Styles – Sam's supposed employer – and asked to speak to Sam.

"Sam?" came the lady's reply. "We ain't got no Sam working here."

Trouble was brewing in Springfield. The following day, I went to the house and Eva answered the door. She informed me (before I could even ask) that Sam was in the bathroom and couldn't come meet me. She quickly handed me the rent – cash – smiled, and closed the door.

Dealer Lesson #4: If your tenant is in the bathroom *every time* you show up to collect the rent, he's not shitting in there.

Looking back, Sam spent a lot of time in the bathroom on days we were there to collect the rent. Low and behold, about five months into their tenancy, the Marvin house was raided for drugs. The Hasselville police kicked in the front door and arrested Sam for dealing crack cocaine. I received a call from the cops that night. They informed me that I might want to get down to the house to lock up and fix the door – which I did the following morning.

When I arrived, I opened the bashed-up door to find Sam standing in the entryway, looking at me. The son of a bitch was already out on bail. I told him he had to get out and that I was going to evict him if he remained past the following weekend.

I felt dirty and ashamed that I had done business with such thugs and I shivered at the thought of our months of ignoring the neighbors' concerns. Sometimes, I guess complaining neighbors can be right. Having felt as if I'd let these neighbors down, I got to work on renovating the house immediately. I would do an exceptional job this time, hoping to get a good tenant in (kind of like penance to the neighborhood, I guess).

I'm not going to get too deep into the horror stories of renovating a crack house (there are plenty of horror stories on subjects like this in Chapter 4), but I'll give you the highlights: They'd built a bar in the main room, which had to be torn down; there was so much trash everywhere that it took me two full days to clean before I could even think about making repairs; and the cabinet under the sink was full (I mean full...there must have been at least 50) of used douche bottles (and I still shudder to think about the awful things that must have gone on in what seems to have been a covert crack/whorehouse).

Oh, and the bathroom sink was clogged. Guess what I found in the p-trap? A little vial of crack that had apparently been forced down with a hair pick. *No wonder the bastard was always in the bathroom*, I remember thinking.

If only that were the end of the story. No, in Springfield, things always seem too complicated. For starters, the cops involved in Sam's bust were later busted themselves for attempting to sell some weed to an undercover policeman. Real brain surgeons, I guess. One of the deputies got 12 years and the head deputy got life. During the resultant trial, it was determined that, among many other places, these crooked cops had planted drugs during the raid of the Marvin house.

But that's still not the end of the story, reader. It wasn't the last I would hear of Sam, either. He would approach me one day while I was renovating another rental property, begging for a second chance, citing how he had been framed and acquitted, and claiming he had found stability in his life by taking a job as a security guard at the nearby Mercedes plant. I almost lost it when I heard he'd been hired to guard luxury cars, but I remained calm when I told him "Hell no."

"Why?" he asked me.

"Because I found crack in the bathroom sink after I kicked you out," I told him. "Regardless of what the court decided, Sam, I know what you are."

You should have seen the poor bastard's face. Priceless. Cowardly, almost. What more can you expect from a crack dealer with a family?

The Violence

Doing our best to turn our attention away from Marvin house for a while, Jackie and I purchased five duplexes and three lots across the street from the local Panty Fair factory. We'll call this the Walnut Street property. We inherited ten existing tenants with the ten rental units (which isn't really all that common...usually you will have to fill an apartment or two). For a couple of months, Jackie and I just collected rent. We were excited because this was a big purchase for us, and it was paying off almost immediately.

By that point, I had gotten pretty good at renovating, so when we had some tenants move out, I decided to take on the challenge of converting this duplex into a 6-bedroom, 2-bathroom home. I put on a new roof, installed new flooring, added central heat and air, textured the walls, and replaced the plumbing, light fixtures, and stainless steel appliances – and (wasn't I proud?) all of that work in just two months. The place looked great.

This was an interesting time for us because there was a national push to move people off welfare and out of housing complexes. It looked like significant reform was on the way. We started getting calls from people from all over the country looking for housing (evidently, Alabama was not participating in the welfare reform program). So we had a flood of people coming from as far away as New Jersey.

Which brings us to our first story from the Walnut Street property...

Though he wasn't our first new tenant there, he was certainly the most dangerous. Actually, when I look back over our entire history of renting, nobody was even close to as dangerous as this guy. A six-year veteran of Hardees's, Christian Turner passed our rental application – and, you know what, looking back, he impressed both of us as an exceptionally nice guy.

When Christian moved in, for some reason, he brought his sister's children with him. Almost immediately, we began to get complaints about him – though I didn't put too much stock into the complaints because the complainers were on my shitlist to begin with. Besides, our criminal and civil background check had turned up clean on Christian.

Violence Lesson #1: Criminal and civil background checks can't predict future behavior.

The future behavior in this case? One day, we got a call from a neighbor of Christian's. The lady said that a car had pulled up to the duplex. The passenger – a man toting a shotgun – jumped out and charged into Christian's unit. "The guy shot one of the kids," the woman said hysterically.

Naturally, I rushed down as soon as I could. Whatever bloodshed had occurred had been cleaned up already, but sure enough, the kitchen door and opposite wall had been peppered with birdshot. Apparently, the kid who had been shot wasn't living with Christian – he was just visiting one of the nephews crashing at the place.

By this time, Christian Turner was already behind on his rent. So I guess you could call this "strike two."

Violence Lesson #2: If "strike two" involves gunplay, then you can pretty much forget about "strike three." He's out.

I sent Christian an eviction notice and even went to Hardees to clear the air. To his credit, he told me he would move. Since I was already there, I decided to get myself a burger and some of those curly fries. As I ate, I perused the newspaper that someone had left on one of the tables. As was my custom, of late, I turned immediately to the section detailing local arrests. There was Christian Turner: robbery and attempted murder.

I looked up from the newspaper and directly at my tenant – the pudgy guy making drinks behind the counter at Hardees. He looked like a mama's boy. Or maybe a singer in the church choir.

Immediately, I left the restaurant and called a local detective, asking him to meet me downtown. Here's what the detective told me:

"Oh yeah, that Turner bunch is from White County. They're all a bunch of drug dealers. Didn't you know?"

Violence Lesson #3: Don't just call the county for your background checks. Sometimes, you've just got to call the state. Sometimes, you've got to call the feds.

So here is the robbery and attempted murder story as I read it in the paper: The repo man had decided to pay Christian a visit. His target: the Turner family automobile. Needless to say, Babyface Turner was none too happy about having his car taken away. So he asked the repo guys if they would at least give him a ride to work (they agreed). He then asked if they could wait one minute while he went back in the house to get something he'd forgotten (they agreed). He emerged from the house with a gun (they quivered). He shot once into the ground and demanded that the repo men lower his car and leave it behind (they agreed). He then fired at them until they left (and they did...quickly).

Here's the best part: Christian then went back into the apartment and hung out as if nothing had even happened. The repo guys of course went to the police, who of course arrested him for assault and attempted murder. Fresh copy for tomorrow's paper. Christian even got to go to work the next day and serve me a burger and fries.

Since we were evicting Christian, we got to look forward to meeting him in court. Surprise, surprise, he didn't show up. No matter. As soon as the judge saw the name in question, he told us not to worry about anything. He then ordered the Sheriff to serve the eviction.

Violence Lesson #4: If he's man enough to fire a gun, he's probably child enough to stay long past his welcome.

You guessed it, the Turner family holed up in the unit until the sheriff's deputy came down himself to escort them off the property. It took all day, but they finally got a U-Haul and vacated the property. I didn't want to stay but I knew I had to change the locks. I really couldn't believe the attitude I was getting from this family as I did my work. Let's do a roll call: they hadn't paid rent, the tenant was going to prison, and they still thought I was the devil for kicking them out. Still, I changed the locks and left. If they wanted to vandalize the property, that was fine by me. Better to be vandalized than to be killed.

Funny story, once we were in the clear on the Turner family, we rented the property out to an 80-year-old woman with a younger boyfriend (he was 60). The woman was staying at a nursing home, where the rent was good but the amenities were bad. See, she was allowed to stay there for free, but they wouldn't let her have sex with her boyfriend. So she decided to take out an apartment (and $300 per month) so she and Romeo would have a place to screw.

Violence Lesson #5: A horny old woman is better than a thuggish young man.

And all that action came from just one duplex. We had 4 others on Walnut Street...

The Feuds

One of the other Walnut duplexes – the one on the corner – has always been a keeper in the rental department (because we've never had any trouble whatsoever in keeping it occupied). Really, it was only a hassle when we first purchased the property. That's because when we bought it, we inherited a feud.

Let me just set the stage. In this corner, we've got a carpenter and his wife, Suneetha. And in this corner, we've got May Green, a dishwasher at a local restaurant and the mother of three girls, whom she took good very good care of. So you've got a self-righteous stay-at-home wife (with a husband who works long hours and is rarely home) squaring off against a tough working mother (who works long hours so she can provide for her children). Call that a culture clash. Or a powder keg. Whichever you prefer.

Feud Lesson #1: When you've got many different families living in close proximity to one another, there's no avoiding the occasional spat. *Expect* feuds.

One morning at around 7:30, Jackie and I were getting our twins ready for school when the telephone rang. I answered. It was Sueneetha.

"There's something funny going on around here," she said.

I just chuckled and handed the phone to Jackie.

"Hello, Sueneetha," Jackie said. "What's going on?"

"There's something funny going on. I washed my clothes and they're not the same color as when I put them in the washer."

"Sueneetha," my wife calmly explained, "it happens to me all the time. Wash darks with lights and the colors will run together. Maybe use Clorox on the whites."

Sueneetha said okay and hung up.

Feud Lesson #2: If *anything* goes wrong – even things that have nothing to do with the feud itself – the complainer will do everything they can to link the problem to their rival.

Despite these backhand digs at May, Jackie liked Sueneetha and was always very patient with her – which was a good thing because Sueneetha would call her about once a month just to talk. I guess she needed someone to vent to because her husband was a more driven kind of guy who took his carpentry seriously – he had a good reputation for being very professional; plus, much to my delight, he was always good for the rent.

But now let's get some feuding done:

One day, May Green called us in tears. We had learned from the previous owner of the duplex that, for years, she had been complaining about the knocking coming from the other side of the common wall between the units. She had always claimed that Sueneetha had a "guest" that was responsible for the noise. By this latest call, I was fed up with the accusations. So, one evening, I went over and listened with May. Low and behold, there was tapping on the wall.

"See!" May said triumphantly. "It's the guest!"

I went next door to confront Sueneetha and her "guest." I knew that if I didn't put a stop to this noise, Jackie and I would never get any sleep. We'd be fielding calls from May at all hours of the night.

When I stepped inside the unit (the "guest" opened the door), I could hear the carpenter and his wife cussing at one another in the other room. So I asked the guest what the knocking was all about. He of course denied everything.

I went back to tell May that I had straightened everything out (it was only a slight lie, I figure, since talking to problem tenants occasionally *does* solve problems). At that moment, May started crying. She led me back over to the common wall and pointed at these empty, tiny picture frame nails. Then, she pointed at the floor below the wall. There sat several nicely framed paintings. I could tell that they were prints, but they obviously still meant a great deal to May. They were, after all, the only decorations in the entire house. Looking very disappointed in me, May then led me back out the door.

"I hope they don't fall again," she said sadly.

As I walked down the driveway, I could hear the carpenter screaming at Sueneetha. What a mess.

The next morning, I went back to May's apartment and told her that I wanted to re-hang her paintings. She let me inside. I removed the unstable framing nails from the sheetrock and replaced them with sturdy screws that I bore into the studs supporting the wall. They weren't going to fall anymore.

Feud Lesson #3: Sometimes, no matter how ridiculous the complaint may be, you just have to intervene.

I never had another complaint about the tapping on the wall. I guess every time those pretty pictures fell, it just about broke May's heart.

I've provided this story for good reason, reader. Feuds can get ugly, yes (and I've got a mountain of feud stories that are dirtier and more bizarre), but they can also simmer just beneath the surface. Many times, feuds will spark or continue over the simplest of things. And as I said, as a landlord, stepping into the fray is often the only way to resolve things. You have to be part moderator in order to do this job. Sometimes, all a moderator has to do is show up.

As an aside, given her career and obvious financial needs, I have no idea how May paid her rent. But she would coordinate with Jackie and pay in full every month. We really liked May and carried a lot of respect for her. That's why it was so depressing when she died of cancer. See, when I first met her, May had a belly that looked swollen. I assumed she was pregnant. I guess that's what she had been assuming, too, because it came as quite a shock to all of us when the doctor diagnosed her with stomach cancer. She passed away not long after hearing the news.

I remember the day some of her relatives came to pick up those poor young girls. The three of them had to be split up and went home with different families. It was devastatingly sad, that afternoon. To this day, I can't help but think about May. She was a proud lady who did the best she could. I don't know if the youngest daughters will remember her, but if they do, I hope they recall the dignified lady we had the pleasure of knowing and doing business with.

See, not all parties involved in feuds are necessarily terrible people. Sometimes, even the most honorable can get caught up in petty squabbles. And I guess that's **Lesson #4.**

The Background Check Forms

I'd like to close this whole sprawling chapter with an overarching lesson, if I could. What you've gotten so far is a nice cross-section of what it's like to deal with low income tenants – and believe it or not, reader, you've basically gotten the censored version. You wouldn't believe the drugs, the abuse, the sex, the drama, the complaints, or the thuggery if I provided it all in full. Plus, if I were to share every seedy story I've encountered, this chapter alone would be a full hundred pages long. Besides, there's plenty more dirty laundry to come...

But let's wrap up this low income tenants chapter with a lesson in background check forms. Even from the beginning, Jackie and I employed background checks on all our tenants. Handshakes and smiles just don't work (particularly when dealing with housing that might appeal to people with low incomes). The only trouble was, when we jumped in with both feet, we didn't realize how damned detailed the forms needed to be or how unbelievably exhausting the digging.

I remember the day we realized it was time for a change. In the early days, we had just required proof of employment and income for tenancy. But after a long string of tenants that burned us on the rent, Jackie and I were drinking coffee and discussing the applications. It was then that we realized income was not enough to justify approval.

In the hopes of avoiding the demolition women and the dealers and the freeloaders and the violence and the feuds, we decided to come up with a form that would allow us to run a civil and criminal background check on our applicants. If you plan on entering this business, I suggest you do the same. Here's how:

1. Go to your local municipal court and ask what kind of clearance you will need to access criminal and civil background information (it's different from county to county).
2. Speak with someone at the housing authority on how to construct your personalized background check form.
3. Develop the form (and be sure to use terminology that your average applicant will understand).
4. Require that all your tenants fill out the form and wait for the results of the check before you allow them to move in.

This little addition to our application helped tremendously. We still have our problem tenants (they're just unavoidable, reader) and we still have to make collection calls, but we haven't had to deal with severe damage or drug issues since.

And remember, if you ever get to the point where you find yourself asking why you got into this business in the first place, consider this: I eventually managed to sell that cursed property on Marvin Street. Know how much Jackie and I cleared on that deal? $50,000. *That*, reader, is why you got into this business in the first place. Keep your patience through all the hassles and collections and repairs, and you will find yourself in position to get wealthy in a hurry.

But before we can get into all the horror stories on renovating and flipping houses and rental units for profit, we need to address a few other important points: Namely, 1) it's never a good idea to allow your tenants to bring in a spouse or significant other who is not on the lease and 2) the collections process can be a real headache. Read on to discover a few tips on how to overcome these common problems.

Chapter Two

Spouses and Significant Others

Before I get into introducing the general rental disaster that this chapter covers, I'd like to quickly revisit a story from Davis 701B – which, as you'll recall from the previous chapter, is one half of a once-cursed duplex that we continue to manage. We eventually got some good tenants into this place, but before that, we had our share of troubling renters. And a few uninvited guests...

Remember Billie Jean? The one with the honest mother, Virginia? Well, believe it or not, Billie Jean actually paid the first two months' rent on time (and on her own). And she probably would have continued. Except that her boyfriend moved in with her.

Billie Jean's guy had a four-door sedan that he was proud of (what is it with these losers and cars?). He was always talking about how handy he was and that he could fix anything. He was handy all right: sitting on the couch, flipping the remote control, and drinking beer. He was a thug and a wonderful role model for Billie's son, Shawn.

Example #1 on thug role models: This genius boyfriend – a short little runt of a guy – quickly figured out that by crawling into the attic, he could get into the adjacent apartment. So he actually crawled into the neighbor's apartment and stole a speaker from one of the children living there. After some bad noise from the police, we got it all sorted out and I climbed up and fixed the attic situation.

Take this one down, reader: When the cops come, even if it's for the spouse, it's time for the offending tenant to get out.

I followed this lesson to the letter, telling Billie Jean she had to move out. Virginia helped me out on that one, securing her daughter a place in the country. That poor kid Shawn, growing up in the shadow of a worthless thug, would remain in trouble for years to come.

But sad as it is to think about how things were for Shawn, these are the kinds of environments you're getting yourself into, reader. If you're willing to embrace this fact – if you're willing to take the losers and freeloaders and thugs in stride – you'll make a whole lot of money. But if not, it might be best to think about buying into a franchise opportunity or something.

So it should be plainly obvious by now why I kicked off this chapter with the story of Billie Jean's MENSA-level boyfriend. Because it illustrates Chapter 2's primary and central lesson: When the boyfriend or spouse moves in with your tenant (and he's not on the lease), it almost always spells trouble.

This is a pretty hard and fast rule, reader. Looking back, I can't tell you how many times a single woman would be making it, paying the bills, and tending to the children, only to have everything fall apart as soon as the *man* moved in. Invariably, this otherwise excellent tenant would stop paying rent and her credit would go down the tubes. The men would convince the women that the due date on rent was more like a flexible term limit – that they could spend their money on something else now and just pay the rent as soon as they got around to it. Strange line of thinking, but there it is.

Most of the time, it's easy to spot a good-for-nothing boyfriend/husband. Warning sign #1 comes in if they plan from day one to live in the apartment but steadfastly refuse to sign the lease. This could mean one of two things: either their credit is so bad that they assume including their name on the lease would be a deal-breaker or they have no intention of honoring the tenets of the contract to begin with. Either way, you're screwed. Warning sign #2 comes post-signing of the lease. If every time you go over to the unit, you find the offending boyfriend/husband lounging around the couch in his undies, mountains of beer cans at his feet, you've probably got a deadbeat on your hands.

But you know, sometimes, you've got to dig even deeper than those two obvious warning signs. Some loser boyfriends/husbands just have a way of flying under the radar...

Jack of All Trades, Master of...Nothing

Let's move back over to the Walnut Street property for a moment. The following story occurred prior to our renovation of the duplexes into a large 6-bedroom/2-bathroom house. It's a nice illustration of the kind of havoc that can be wreaked by a layabout spouse or significant other.

Lucy James had just signed a lease with us and was getting settled in to her new apartment. In stepped William (or "Bill," as he liked to be called) and their three children. Now in the early days, we had no trouble with this kind of arrangement, but after a while, we learned the hard way that it's best to have both paying tenants on the lease. Still, we let it slide – old Bill was a jack of all trades, after all. He could do anything and everything (which boiled down to "absolutely nothing" once his buzz wore off). Seriously. I never saw him sober.

Anyway, Lucy had gotten a job at a fast food place and Bill supposedly worked nights cleaning some factory I wasn't familiar with. One day, I was working on a unit next door to the James' unit and Billy, Jack of all trades, offered to help me with the painting. Now I'll get into the dangers of letting tenants and neighbors help out with renovation efforts in Chapter 4, but for now, suffice to say that I was short on time, naïve, and glad to have the help. Long story short, I told Bill that I would pay him $50.00 to finish the kitchen. He agreed. I left him to his devices.

You might think you know where I'm going with this story, but stick with me here. There's a twist.

When I came back, believe it or not, it actually did look like Bill had done himself a nice job of painting. So I paid him and went happily on my way. Now here's the twist: What I didn't know was that Bill had hired some kid off the street to do the work for him. The kid he hired? Shawn Lawson, Billie Jean's unfortunate son. Small world.

So, anyway, Bill had hired Shawn and of course not paid him.

Deadbeat Spouse/Significant Other Lesson #1: Deadbeat spouses/significant others tend to stir up trouble with neighbors and other tenants.

It's a strange phenomenon. I guess if you spend all of your days bumming around on the couch, you've got to figure out ways to keep your life interesting. I mean, the TV can only take you so far. Trouble comes calling sooner or later. And the inevitable alcohol problems tend to help spark the fire.

Back to our story. Lucy was greeted at home that evening by a headache she didn't know how to deal with on her own. I know this because Jackie took her hysterical call. Jackie confesses that she can't remember all that was said on the phone, but she distinctly recalls a great deal of rambling regarding Lucy having to take a bat to a boy who was at the unit demanding money and threatening to kill poor Bill. Shawn, with his thuggish role model, had taken to thuggish devices, it seemed.

And where was Bill during all of this? At his night job, of course; most likely working off his hangover.

So I did the only thing you can do in this situation – I got in my truck and went over there to Walnut Street to find out what the hell was going on. When I arrived, Lucy was scared to death, cowering behind the door when I knocked. Funny how quickly that changed when she saw it was me, though. She toughened up and stood right behind me – calling Shawn every name she could think of – as I confronted the bat-wielding boy with the furrowed brow, the paint-spackled fingers, and the apparently empty wallet.

"Let's all calm down," I remember saying. "I paid Bill directly, Shawn. I'll see what I can do about getting you your money."

Well, I found out in short order that Bill had already spent my $50 on booze.

Deadbeat Spouse/Significant Other Lesson #2: Funny how the rent money tends to get tied up each month on booze, drugs, or car repairs.

Anyway, I'm sure Bill needed a drink on his way to work for the evening. Or $50 worth of drink. After a lot of bad noise with this deadbeat husband, I realized that there was no resolving the issue. So I wound up writing Shawn a check for what he felt he was owed and told him never to do any more work for Bill. In fact, I politely asked him never to return to any of my properties.

So that was my first run-in with Bill. He caused a $50 paint job to cost me a hundred.

From there, things just went downhill. We had quite a time collecting from Lucy from that day forward. She was experiencing a collections issue with some lenders (she had bought some furniture on credit, apparently). So each month, we had to beat the furniture people to the door. Bill, on the other hand, was tougher to beat to the door, seeing as how he lived behind it.

On the months that Lucy did pay, she always had this smug look of satisfaction on her face whenever she handed over the rent money. After all, she had worked hard for it. In fact, she had been working for some time, by that point, and tax time had come and gone. I got word that she was expecting some money back from the government – and low and behold, her refund was somewhere north of $2,000. The whole neighborhood heard about that one.

Now would be a good time to mention that neither Lucy nor Billy had any kind of formal education to speak of. The trouble with uneducated folks is that when they come into a large sum of money, they have no idea how to manage it wisely. Their eyes just light up with liquor bottles and cartons of cigarettes and bling. Or used cars. See, at that time all the used car dealers in our area would prepare income taxes for free. This was a nice deal for poor, uneducated folks who couldn't afford to pay to have their taxes done for them; but it was also a nice deal for the grinning salesmen, who would never let one of their tax-prospects off the lot without talking them in to spending their refund money on a down payment for a used car. Of course, by the time the refund checks arrived to the dealers, the hidden costs and late fees would have consumed the entire down payment amount and the uneducated taxpayer would be behind the eight-ball.

Of course I mention this because Lucy and Bill were two of the unfortunate many who took advantage of the free taxes deal. One evening, Jackie and I drove up to collect the rent and there was a 1975 Ford LTD pulled up close to their apartment door. I'm sure it was a grand car in its day, but at the time, it was over 20 years old. Bill was sitting in the back seat, drinking and listening to the radio. I don't think he ever knew we stopped by.

Deadbeat Spouse/Significant Other Lesson #3: If there's a car in the yard, you're in trouble.

I told Lucy that the car was a bad idea – that it would eventually break down and be too expensive to operate. I was right. Too right. From the very first expense (they didn't even have enough money for proper tags), their financial backs were broken. Of course, it didn't help that old William started getting tickets for DUI, as well. The funniest part is what Billy would do during the day while his doting wife was at work. He would wheel his LTD out to the housing projects and tell all the street ladies that he was loaded. I guess he became the projects' own ladies man.

Fortunately for all parties involved, the car broke down shortly after purchase and was towed away.

Domestic Violence (Of All Sorts)

Stay with me here, because I'm about to rattle off a couple quick stories about domestic abuse – starring three very unlikely parties. Maybe I should call this segment, "The Toddler, the Neighbor, and the Knife." Has a nice ring to it...

The following stories take place at the property that we'll call 807 Montgomery Street. This was an old house we had recently purchased. The place had a big porch, which we figured would either be a great selling point for elderly tenants or thuggish tenants. Unfortunately, we usually got the latter. But the greatest domestic violence stories occurred not in the house, but in the rectangular store that came attached. See, the store had been converted into two one-bedroom efficiency apartments. Having fixed them up nicely, Jackie and I were excited about getting them rented. We didn't have any trouble with filling the space. We did, however, have plenty of trouble with the *people* who would fill it.

Anyway, let's get started with the toddler.

By this time, we also owned a house on Hunter Street that we were renting out to a nice elderly couple. The elderly couple didn't care much for their son Eli or his wife Brenda, but they did enjoy the company of their only grandson – more than I would come to enjoy his company, anyway. So they would ask Jackie and me if we would rent to their son and his wife one of the efficiency apartments that we had just opened up for lease. They assured us that they would make sure we got our money each month. On that condition, we agreed.

I remember the first time I met this grandson, the little shit. I had come over to complete a work request on the gas-powered wall-unit heater. I was clanking away on the thing when the precious little tike came waddling up to me, obviously carrying a shitty load in his diaper and ominously carrying a toy plastic baseball bat in his hand. You can see where this is going. The smelly grandson immediately started hitting me in the back with the bat. I just sighed and kept working while the brat continued to wail on me. I did my best to keep my rage from building – passing the time between each crashing blow by thinking about my sons when they were little (I had twins, after all, I was used to this kind of stuff) – but this kid just kept hammering his point home.

When it became clear to the toddler that I wasn't going to react to just hitting, he turned to insults, as well. Picture this: a grown man huddled in the corner of an efficiency apartment, taking savage blows from a child with a toy bat. Now picture this: after each strike, the toddler starts calling the grown man "bitch." Yeah. With the kid's parents and grandparents talking in the far corner of the room, here I am balled up with a wrench in my hand, suffering through, "*Whack!* Bitch! *Whack!* Bitch!"

Eventually, the little bundle of joy's grandmother walked over to see how things were going.

"I'm having a hard time with this little fella," I said, deadpan. "He's been whacking me and calling me a bitch."

Of course, in Grandma's mind, the child could do no wrong – so instead, she took her anger out on her son, Eli. "Come get this baby!" she barked. "He's cussing out the landlord."

Luckily, by the time Eli got up the energy to do anything about it, I was finished with the heater. So I left.

Domestic Violence Lesson #1: In case you hadn't already noticed, asshole spouses/significant others tend to raise asshole children.

Let's shift gears and talk about the parents of this pint-sized treasure, shall we? Eli was a short, paunchy little guy who apparently looked in the mirror and saw a beautiful black man. Brenda, meanwhile, was a chubby, bleach-blonde white girl who talked with startling ghetto sound. She worked two jobs while Prince Eli spent his days lying on the couch. He led the proverbial double life. During the day, he would drink with all of the drunkards and thugs in the neighborhood. Then, at night, he wouldn't let them in the house, pretending like he didn't even know them.

Well, when you piss off street people – as Eli frequently did by locking up his doors – they tend to react like they always do: with violence. Violence, in this case, manifested itself in a not-so-original way. Namely, rocks would come flying through Eli and Brenda's front window. If I had to guess, I'd say that I replaced the same window pane about three times before I gave up and asked Allen (my glass-man) if there was something else that I could use. He told me that I could replace it with a new kind of plastic pane called LEXan, but that it would cost me $100. I bit the bullet and bought the pane.

About a week later, I heard a story that made me laugh so hard I almost wet myself. Apparently, the guy who had been breaking the window managed to knock himself out when he tried throwing a brick at the LEXan. The brick bounced back and brained him. So that's one way to solve a problem.

Plastic bats and bouncing bricks aside, domestic violence can sometimes get pretty nasty. And it always seems to happen to couples where only one tenant is on the lease. Take the other efficiency tenants at Montgomery Street, for example...

One tenant seemed like a nice lady with a decent job at Wal-Mart. I don't recall her name, so we'll just call her "Wal-Mart Lady." Wal-Mart Lady's financial records indicated that she could afford the apartment, anyway, which was music to mine and Jackie's ears. Well it's the same old song, reader. All was well until Wal-Mart Lady let her baby's daddy move in. I don't recall his name, either (call it selective memory loss), so let's just call him "Baby Daddy." Anyway, Baby Daddy was a good-looking guy – purportedly a fireman and a nice, courteous, standup guy – who often wore a little diamond earring.

Well, surprise, surprise, this nice, courteous, standup guy began showing up in the police reports that Jackie and I checked routinely. The charges? Domestic violence. What did we do about it? Nothing. Until one night, anyway...

We received the call in the late evening, I remember. Baby Daddy had threatened to choke Eunice, a young lady living in one of the nearby duplexes that we owned. That's bad enough, but apparently Eunice also happened to be packing a knife. Well, the attempted choking led to a successful stabbing. Baby Daddy survived the wound, but he used his new lease on life to try to have *her* arrested. Genius.

The cops didn't arrest Eunice (seeing as how she was only defending herself), but they didn't arrest Baby Daddy, either. Still, that was enough for us. Wal-Mart Lady had to go. And to her credit, she got out the following weekend. I also told Eunice that our business was over and that she needed to get out. Reluctantly, she followed suit.

Sometimes, It's the Women...
Let's introduce this one like they do all those trashy and hilarious daytime courtroom TV shows:

He was the good son of the famous Ms. Patsy. She was a skinny little woman who bitched about anything and everything. As the plaintiff claims, Ms. Margaret Price would drink Mr. Chucky Benson out of house and home.

While this story may represent a cautionary tale about how you can't trust female tagalong tenants either, the call that would begin this particular nightmare would come from the future man of the house, Charles "Chucky" Benson. Jackie tells me that when Chucky first called to ask about an apartment, he was slurring his words. Not a good sign. But still, we were desperate for a tenant.

Jackie had a hard time understanding Chucky, but she finally got him to spell out where he worked. Turned out, it was a nearby tire store (and he claimed to have been working there for more than twenty years). Naturally, that story seemed unlikely, so Jackie asked Chucky to stay put – that she would be over to the store in twenty minutes to go over the details.

Jackie informs me that she liked Chucky from the moment she first saw him in that tire store. He was a slender man with an infectious smile (despite the fact that he was missing literally all of his teeth). Jackie shook his hand and they went over to a small table in the back office, where they sat down to go over the rental application.

As you do, Jackie asked Chucky if he had any credit references.

"No," he said. "I pay cash for everything."

Warning bells, reader.

"But I'll pay for six months in advance, if that'll help. I'd hate to get behind on the rent."

The warning bells grow softer, reader, more distant.

Jackie confesses that she almost fell out of her chair. She nodded vigorously and completed the lease, which Chucky signed.

The honest tire store worker smiled as he stood. "Hold on a minute," he said. "I'll be right back with the deposit and the rent."

They shook hands and then went together to the back of the store. Once there, Chucky gave my wife the deposit, plus six months' rent. "I don't have a checking account," he confessed, "so on the third of every month, come by the store to get your rent."

Jackie also confesses that, by this point, it was difficult for her to keep from grinning like a mental patient. She informed Chucky that he was paid up until June – and that she would see him July 3rd at the tire store. Then, she dropped the bombshell: "Please don't hesitate to call if there are any problems at the apartment."

Jackie went directly from the tire store to the bank. I remember the excitement in her face when she told me she had six months' advanced rent from the most amazing tire guy she had ever met.

Unfortunately, when Chucky moved in, he brought his girlfriend, Margret Price. She took Jackie's offer at calling in the event of apartment-related problems a little too literally. I'd be putting it mildly if I said that she bitched about anything and everything. If I asked her how she liked something in the apartment, her response was always the same: "I hate it...hate it." But beside the fact that we both liked and admired Chucky, I managed to overlook her moodiness because I thought she might be suffering from a drug and/or alcohol problem. Boy, was I right.

Margaret was just about the nastiest woman I've ever seen. She kept a surprisingly clean house, but looked like a dirty little crackhead. She would stumble around drunk, slurring her words. Her hair was always sticking straight up. Sometimes, she'd even have a piece of lint or paper sticking to it.

One time, Chucky called and asked me to fix a leak under the kitchen sink. So I knocked on the door and Margaret slurred to come in.

"Hi," I said. "Chucky called about the sink."

She was sitting in the living room with four of her fat-ass girlfriends, all of them drinking and laughing. I paid no attention to them, instead going straight in to fix the sink, which I did as quickly as possible. On my way out, I walked by and told Margaret that I had finished with the sink.

"But are you finished with *me*?" she asked (in just about the creepiest voice I've ever heard.)

I grimaced, not wanting to imagine what she must have been telling that gaggle of drunken women. Poor Chucky. As it turned out, this loser girlfriend and her hefty friends were the very reasons that Jackie had to pick up the rent money at the tire store every month. Chucky just couldn't keep his money at home. Otherwise, Margaret would spend it all on drugs and alcohol.

Chucky's story has a sad ending, reader. Margaret's story, meanwhile, would live on in complicated fashion (and we'll get to that portion of the show in the next chapter on collections).

One day at work, Chucky had a devastating stroke. Margaret looked after Chucky for a couple of months. During this time, while he was on his death bed, she arranged for a preacher to come by the apartment and marry them. So Margaret Price was now Margaret Lawson. Trouble.

Chucky passed on – and may he rest in peace because the fight started over his 401(k) and other benefits not a minute after his passing. But more on that drama later...

Divorce, Dispute, Adultery, Etc.

We were constantly dealing with tenants in crisis. Couples going through a divorce are difficult to handle. You really feel bad for them and kind of rejoice if they manage to get it back together. But of course that rarely happens.

One incident that comes to mind involves a nurse who was leaving her husband because he had an affair. Just to be cute, let's call her Betty. And let's call him Ronald. Anyway, I remember that, one night, Ronald kicked the door in and I had to fix it. Betty called the cops on him, but didn't prosecute. There's a lesson in this:

D, D, and A Lesson #1: Abused spouses will rarely prosecute. If your property is involved, don't be afraid to step in and do it for them.

I followed Lesson #1 and told Nurse Betty that I would prosecute her husband if he ever came back on my property. But even though he was supposedly beating her and harassing her, she decided to take him back.

As a condition of our little spoken agreement, Betty and Ronald had to go. So Jackie let the nurse out of her lease. Sometimes, you have to make concessions if you want to get people to leave. I dropped by while they were packing up to leave, noticing that they had been kind enough to leave a circular burn in the middle of the living room carpet. Jackie and I found out later that the burn was from when Ronald, being the levelheaded douchebag that he was, tried to burn up their wedding pictures on our floor.

Credit where credit is due: Nurse Betty paid for the damaged carpet.

This is just one story in a long line of domestic abuse cases, reader. In fact, if you plan on going into this business, expect the horrifying problem to come up a lot. It might be because we knew an inordinate number of women suffering from abuse (Jackie worked at the local women's abuse center in her free time), but I don't think so. I think it's just a part of the landlording game.

Anyway, in some cases, we would be renting an apartment to a woman in the hopes of helping her start her life over after leaving an abusive husband/boyfriend. This was always tough on us, though, because the woman would almost always allow the bastard in question back into her life and onto our property. The boyfriend/husband would often cause property damage and disturb neighbors. Whenever this happened, I found myself feeling less sorry for them.

That may seem like a harsh thing to say, but reader, you have to understand that, from my point of view, I felt a responsibility to protect the other tenants. So when more and more abused women kept bringing in their loser significant others, I became a little cynical and cautious when dealing with them in the future. Needless to say, I learned some lessons that changed my views on domestic violence...at least for now.

So in any case, we rented an apartment to a schoolteacher named Thelma Peters. She was a tiny young woman, maybe weighing 95 pounds. She was a nice tenant, quiet and unassuming, always paid the rent on time…for about six months. Then she started dating a skinny guy named Melvin. Old Melvin was attending the university nearby. He was about 6'3" and clearly thought he was pretty as hell. The bumper of his car proudly carried a red sticker that read "Dirt Road Gangster." What a twit.

The first time I laid eyes on my new (and unwelcome) tenant, he was pulling his car into the front yard of the apartment complex we owned (more on dealing with apartment complex tenants later, by the way). He'd pulled the car up into the grass so he could wash it. Here's the fun part: he had to run a hose all the way from the back of the building (where their water spigot was located) to the front yard (where the imbecile was getting some scrubbing and hosing done). Now this was quite a distance, reader. I'm thinking he must have had nine or more hoses connected together.

As if that wasn't inconsiderate enough, Melvin apparently decided that, in future, my front yard would become his personal parking space. Since he didn't have a job, his car was always there, too. Actually, I take that back. He did have a job: cleaning that stupid-ass neon green LTD. Many times, I would drive up to see him washing that damn car, his rap music blasting. Rap music might be fine for some people, but not for me. Plus, regardless of your feelings on the genre, you have to admit that the lyrics are dirty as hell. Blaring words like that into public space just isn't right. In Melvin's case, it was downright terrible.

One day, I saw that his car was parked in the yard, as usual. Well, I'd had enough by this point. So I knocked on Thelma's door. When the lout didn't answer, I left a note on his car stating that we did not allow the washing of automobiles in the front yard or on the sidewalks.

Later that afternoon, I went to have a talk with Thelma. She was pregnant now, so I was sure to be delicate with her. Calmly and politely, I asked her to please have the car removed from the front yard. The car remained in place for another twelve hours, but I guess Melvin eventually worked up the energy to get off his ass and move it, because the next day, it was gone.

You can probably see where this is going...

Two days later, that piss-green LTD was back in the front yard.

This might not seem like a big deal, but it is, reader. You've got to worry about the aesthetics of the situation or the rest of your tenants start to bitch. Plus, having to tend to all that water from car washing is a real hassle. Picture a nice apartment complex, landscaped, with a parking lot and nice sidewalks leading up to the front doors. It's quiet in the afternoon because everyone is working. Now picture a bright green LTD sitting about ten feet away from the front door, straddling the sidewalk and grass. Forget aesthetics; the idea that anyone could think it okay to park in such a way is completely absurd.

I guess old Melvin thought I was trying him, because every couple of days, he would have that ridiculous car of his back in the front yard. So when reasoning with him didn't work, we started searching for dirt. You'll be blown away by this little revelation, reader, I know, but as soon as Jackie began to investigate him, she discovered that Melvin had been in trouble with the law. Among other things, he had been hauled in for domestic violence incidents. To our shock and dismay, our address was listed on a few of the incident reports. Thelma was getting beat up on our property and she wasn't even telling us.

So we intervened. I filled out trespassing warnings on him. We attempted a restraining order. Thelma was no help.

For a few more months, these two lovebirds stayed together, becoming hideous creatures, wraiths of their former selves. And they were bringing an innocent child into this mess...

Eventually, we got a break with Melvin when he took up with another girl around the six-month point of her pregnancy. I guess ole Melvin thought Thelma had gotten fat and let herself go. Of course we felt bad for Thelma, being pregnant, tiny, and alone, but at least she wasn't getting beat up anymore. Naturally, Jackie and I were concerned about Thelma, so we worked with her to make sure she had the rent paid so she at least had shelter. And we always made sure it was Jackie contacting her. She couldn't stand me – I think that, deep down, it's because she blamed me for her loser fiancé leaving her.

Well, as these things often work out, Melvin managed to get his new girlfriend pregnant, as well. Apparently feeling that she couldn't provide for him any longer in her state, he moved back in with Thelma, now a proud but desperate mother. So we were graced with old Melvin's presence once again.

I bet you can guess how I knew of his return. Yep, his car was parked in the front yard.

So now Thelma had to take care of her baby and her thug. It didn't take her long to lose track of one of them: the thug. The cops had to pay a visit to their unit again. This time, we received word of the incident.

That was it for me. I told Thelma that she was either going to have to leave or make him leave. One or the other. I stressed that we had done all we could do to help her out, but that now it was up to her.

Jackie gave her the number at the domestic violence shelter and told her about the services she could expect to receive there. I reminded Thelma that we had both signed trespassing warnings against Melvin.

"Okay," she said adamantly. "I'll tell Melvin to leave." She then handed me the rent check.

Later that afternoon, the thug called me and told me to bring his money back.

I laughed a little, though I tried to hide it over the phone. "You want me to bring back the rent money?" I asked.

"Yeah," he said, all tough-guy-like. "I gave her the money and it's my money and I want it back!"

"What about your baby?" I asked. "Aren't you worried about providing shelter for your baby?"

"I want my money back," he yelled.

Naturally, a fight between the two lovebirds broke out. In Thelma's apartment. All this despite the fact that we had changed the locks on the doors so Thelma didn't have to let him in. All this despite the fact that Thelma had promised us she would never let him in the building again.

"Let me speak to Thelma," I barked into the phone.

Melvin handed it over. "Hello?" she squeaked.

"What's going on?" I asked her. "I thought we had a deal."

"We do," she whispered, crying. "He won't leave."

"I'll be there in five minutes," I said.

While I got ready to go take care of business, Jackie called a policeman she knew from her work at the domestic violence shelter. The cop met me at the door. We knocked, and when Thelma answered, I could immediately tell that they had been fighting. She had a black eye.

I asked Melvin to leave, but he was stretched out on the couch and refused to move. He said he wasn't leaving because it had been he who had paid me the rent.

"You don't live here," I said to him. Then, I turned to the officer and said, "This apartment is leased solely to Thelma. He's trespassing here."

The policeman apparently knew Melvin from prior calls, because he called him by name when he told him to get out.

Melvin actually jumped up off the couch and made a show of bowing to the officer. But when the policeman took his elbow, Melvin snatched it away. But being as scrawny as he was, it didn't take much of a struggle before he started to fall in line. He spent the entire time mumbling angrily, but he finally got his stuff together and got in the car. The kindhearted man that he is, he was nice enough to gun his engine and leave a giant bald spot in my yard.

The loser now gone, the policeman did his best to get a report from Thelma, but she wouldn't say anything. She just closed the door on us. The cop and I looked at each other and just shook our heads.

Something must have snapped in me that day, because my feelings on domestic abuse changed. I felt betrayed by Thelma. No matter how hard we tried to help and how patient we were with her, she would keep letting the gangster back into her life. I could tell she hated me (she never smiled or responded to anything I said), but still. That's no excuse to take a beating.

It was an epiphany that I had that day. Just like Thelma was with Melvin, Jackie and I had spent all kinds of time making excuses for our tenant's inexcusable behavior. Our desire to overlook her flaws as a renter put everyone in the complex at risk. Our inability to deal directly with the problem led to damage to our property, as well.

The Saturday following the incident with the policeman, Thelma and Melvin left the apartment in the middle of the night. They loaded up a truck and she skipped out on her lease. This affected me profoundly. Still, we were relieved that they were gone.

Jackie rented an apartment to a short, bald fellow who had taken a job at the Hasselville Dam. Wallace. A real Southern success story. I say this because Wallace was already drawing a pension from the US Army and now found employ with the federal government. He must have had thousands of dollars to party on each month. Anyway, it was a federal job that brought him to Hasselville from Blounte County. Meanwhile, his wife had stayed behind to live in Moundeville.

Now Wallace loved to talk. His favorite subject when talking to me? Women. Specifically, female anatomy. I thought this was strange, given that I knew Wallace to be married.

But I don't think I was ever at the apartment complex without seeing a woman knocking on old Wallace's door. I often found myself in Wallace's apartment, too, because he was one of those tenants who would always pay rent, but then demand some kind of extra service or update on the apartment.

One day, I was in doing some service because Wallace wasn't satisfied with the performance of one of the electric eyes on his stove. So I sat on the kitchen floor, working on the thing, when someone knocked on the kitchen door. Before I could answer, the door came flying open. When I looked up, I saw a clearly drunken woman in a flower-print skirt and a floppy hat. She stumbled straight into the kitchen, looking very much like a streetwalker.

"Wait a minute," I said as she headed toward the living room. "Wallace," I hollered.

"Come on up, baby," Wallace yelled back down.

After a few minutes, Wallace came downstairs into the kitchen, grinning. He stuck his head through the kitchen door, looking to the left and to the right before speaking. "She got some good pussy," he said enthusiastically. Then, he went back upstairs.

I went straight back to work, trying to forget about what had just happened. Cringing, I realized that I would need to go pick up a part for the stove, which meant I would have to return the next day to complete the repair.

The next day, Wallace opened the door for me. I immediately noticed his black eye.

"What happened?" I asked.

"I took that nice lady you met yesterday to a picnic," he explained. "Her ex-boyfriend was there."

"Looks like he popped you pretty good," I said.

"Oh, he didn't do it," he said. "She did."

Seems she had taken the side of the ex in the epic fight.

Now that's not even the funny part. Here's the funny part: I hadn't even started to install the new electric eye when the lady knocked on the door. Drunk.

"Go on upstairs," Wallace told her. And she did as she was asked.

"Wallace," I said, "I know this isn't any of my business, but that lady's crazy. You're gonna get stabbed or killed if you don't leave her alone."

He just waved me off. "She got some good pussy," he said.

He went upstairs and I let myself out.

A couple of days later, when I was reading the paper, I saw a headline about a Hasselville man who'd been stabbed in Blounte County by a woman and died on the way to the hospital. Yep. Wallace.

I called Jackie and she was floored. "You told him a week ago that this would happen," she said. "He should've taken your advice."

I really couldn't believe it was true. So my wife and I went to his apartment. No one there. We contacted his work and they confirmed the article. His wife, meanwhile, didn't seem to care.

"We'll come down and get what we can from the apartment," she said.

Two weeks later, we checked up on the progress of the move and found that Wallace's wife didn't want the furniture. I called and left her a message explaining that we would be happy to deliver it to her. She called back and said that a relative in Sweetwater could use the furniture.

So Jackie and the boys helped me load up the furniture. We drove it to a trailer hidden down a goat trail of a road near Sweetwater. We backed up to the trailer and a couple of women helped us unload onto the grass in front of the trailer. Jackie and the women stood in front of the furniture and belongings and I took a picture. Jackie had them sign a receipt of the belongings. Jackie gave them a hug and wished them well. Then we got into the truck and left.

We managed to clear the apartment and get it ready for the next tenant within three weeks of Wallace's death. I was relieved. I would have felt bad for Wallace, but it was obvious that his wife and kids didn't care. Unfortunately, this wouldn't be the last time we would deal with the death of one of our tenants, either...

Chapter Three

Resident Death

As you've already seen here and there, reader, tenants are subject to all of the strictures and shortcomings that the rest of us are. One of them, believe it or not, includes death. The question isn't whether you'll have a tenant die on you at some point; the question is how you'll respond to it.

Sometimes, responses have to come before you even get started. For example, when we bought our 22-unit apartment complex, we inherited a fully furnished unit. The unit was packed with a woman's personal possessions. She'd died eight months prior. The manager had given the key to her attorney, who had in turn given it to one of her sons. If the son took anything, it must have been small, because the unit was full of furniture, a television, clothes, and other possessions.

Resident Death Lesson #1: Plan on paying for a storage unit from time to time.

111

Jackie and I started to rent a storage unit and haul the belongings over there, but instead, we decided to ignore Lesson #1 and avoid the extra expense at all costs. So my wife made a call to the woman's attorney. He advised her to just get rid of it.

I figured it was a fair deal, so I inspected the furniture and things to see if it was of any value. The woman had an extensive collection of vinyl LPs that I thought might be worth something. But then I went on eBay and found that records, these days, are sold in packs of 100 for mere dollars – basically not worth much more than the shipping costs. All of the furniture was worn out and the electronics were obsolete or didn't work. So I just made a video of the stuff and filed it for future reference, if needed.

Jackie called our friends Rusty and Ms. Beth to come and take whatever they wanted. Ms. Beth had a field day. It took them about three days, but they cleared the whole apartment.

I was relieved to have the unit cleared and ready for a tenant, but at the same time, I knew that we would now have to figure on putting a death clause in our lease, specifying that we would immediately put any furniture and possessions into storage upon death and store it for three months. I never did get the clause finished, though, figuring it would be best just to work with family, even if it meant that we had to deliver to them.

But even with that out of the way, it would be sooner than we would hope before we would have to deal with it again.

Jackie rented the apartment across the street to a single woman named Sadie. I had a couple of nice conversations with her during an electrical repair, and later, a water heater repair. She was very sweet and thoughtful, that Sadie, but had an air of loneliness about her. After a couple of months, her rent was late, which was very unusual for her. She would have called if she had a problem, so we assumed the worst.

We were right.

Jackie called and a family member answered her phone, informing my wife that Sadie had had a heart attack.

Jackie went to the hospital and checked up on her. Obviously, since she was in the hospital – and hospitals are ridiculously expensive – Sadie wouldn't be able to cover the rent each month. So we worked out a reasonable payment plan that worked for her.

But Sadie was having a tough time and really couldn't work anymore. Her doctor wanted to perform a risky (and expensive) surgery, but she elected not to have it, instead deciding to check out of the hospital. From the day she was discharged, Jackie would go by Sadie's apartment and check on her – mostly because she enjoyed talking to her. Jackie said it was always sad to leave her side because she would just sit on the couch all alone, smoking away, and say goodbye.

Yes, it was the cigarettes that had caused the problem, but she couldn't put them down. This was especially painful for me to watch because my father struggled with lung damage from smoking. He was in and out of the hospital for about nine years. His heart was strong, but he couldn't get any air. His death involved terrible suffering and that was difficult for all of us to bear.

About three months after Sadie in her door when they responded to a 911 call. The ambulance had taken her to the hospital, but the police wanted me to secure the apartment. When I got there, they told me that Sadie had called 911 because she couldn't get any air. When the ambulance arrived, they found her lying on the living room floor.

The jam had split on the door when they'd kicked it in, but I told the police that I would take care of everything.

Resident Death Lesson #2: Don't just expect to repair kicked-in doors following medical emergencies. Expect to clean up messes you can't imagine.

I put a screw through the busted jam and pulled it back together so the lock would engage. I then walked through the apartment. I found a foamy trail of blood that traced back to her bedside. I grabbed a paper towel and dabbed up the foam. It disgusts me even to type this, but it has to be done: there were pieces of pink lung tissue in the mess, as well. I could only imagine her coughing and struggling so hard to get air that she tore part of her lungs out. Unable to think about anything else but cleaning the place up, I went to the nearby convenience store and bought carpet cleaner. When I returned I got to work scrubbing the stains.

The next morning, we learned that Sadie had died.

Broken up about it though we were, we had little choice but to keep working on the unit. So Jackie called Buddy, a carpet cleaner. And Buddy rushed over to work on the stains.

Jackie and I talk about Sadie to this day. We can't help but feel sad and wish we could have stayed longer on the days that she felt like talking. I hope that wherever she is now, she isn't lonely.

I can't imagine the fear and the horrifying struggle to face death alone.

A couple of weeks later, when I was working on the unit, I swear I could still see traces of blood. I was so overwhelmed that I couldn't do much more than just sit on the floor. I wasn't crying – I think that part of me is long gone – but I was full of intense sorrow for the kind lady that had died alone. I guess I have always tried to stay busy to keep from facing these feelings. But sometimes, reader, you just can't outrun them.

By the time I finally got up, it was dark.

It wouldn't be the last time I would feel this way, either.

One day, we ran into a woman who worked at the kidney dialysis center who said she knew an elderly man, Lester, who needed an apartment. Lester received disability checks, but was also under the employ of the center. We agreed to allow him to move into the complex.

One of Lester's first acts as our tenant was to put a bench outside to the left of his front door. He loved to sit there all day.

Unfortunately, Lester was in bad shape. He had a huge stitch-mark down his chest from open-heart surgery. He also had all kinds of ports on his body for plugging in the dialysis machine. On his bench, he would sit and smoke cigarettes all day. It really gave those apartments a "projects" look. I just hated people sitting outside in front of the doors. Not only did it look bad, it invited trouble, as well. So I finally got him to move the bench to his back patio, where no one would see him.

Lester's main problem wasn't his health, either. It was his wife, Sabritha. She wore lots of makeup and loved to walk the streets – to the point where she had gained notoriety in Hasselville. I don't know her whole story, but I definitely didn't want her turning tricks from the bench at the apartment complex.

Lester's health went downhill because he often had surgery to find the veins for the dialysis treatments. One day, he just didn't come back. I called the dialysis center to find out how he was and they said he had passed away. I immediately went to check on his unit and found that everything was gone. His next of kin had cleared the apartment before I even knew about the death. So I just changed the locks and cleaned the unit.

The death of a tenant puts the landlord in a situation beyond their pay grade. While you often have to be the bearer of bad news – in cases of eviction – when a tenant dies, sometimes you feel like you're the doctor, the coroner, or even the next of kin. The key to making this situation easier – if that's at all possible – is to plan for the inevitable. You'll no doubt be left with a little extra furniture. Sometimes, you will be left with a tenant who owes you money. And money, as we all know, is tough enough to collect.

Chapter Four

Collections

In Chapter 2, you were introduced to the story of poor Chucky and money-grubbing Margaret. I cut the story off midstream for good reason: the tail end serves as the perfect anecdote to begin our chapter on Collections. Before I begin with that, though, let's just cut to the heart of the matter on collecting rent and back-rent.

Collections Lesson #1: If you've never seen the inside of a courtroom, plan on that changing.

Yes, reader, if you want to make your No Money Down millions, expect to get your hands dirty in the courthouse. You'll stand before judges from time to time. You'll plead your completely logical case against a number of imbeciles with weak claims and grievances. You'll spend your share on legal fees.

But anyway, enough of that. Let's talk about Margaret...

Several months after Chucky's untimely death, Margaret was way behind on the rent. But she kept assuring Jackie that she was about to receive a large check from Chucky's benefits and would then be able to quickly catch up. Evidently, Chucky's sister (also named Margaret Lawson), had stolen a benefits check and cashed it before the newly ordained Margaret Price/Lawson could get her hands on it. Margeret Price/Lawson informed Jackie that she was suing for this money and would recover it in short order. She even gave Jackie her attorney's telephone number, just so my wife could clear the air and get her peace of mind.

Only trouble was that Margaret was about $2,500 in the hole. In other words, we were way past the time of patience. So Jackie decided to speak to the attorney, who assured her that Margaret would receive a check any day now. As I said, we were beyond patience, so Jackie informed this lawyer that we would be taking the case of Margaret Price's back-rent to court. We figured that even if Margaret got the money she was owed, she wouldn't pay us anyway. It would all get blown on drugs and booze.

Collections Lesson #2: Tenants owing money will give you all kinds of sob stories about why they don't have your money; sometimes you just have to head trouble off at the pass.

The hearing was a disaster. The judge extended Margaret's stay for an additional 30 days, citing her current legal predicament as justification for the extension. Hell, let's just jump straight into Lesson #3...

Collections Lesson #3: Sometimes, no matter how ridiculous your tenants' claims may be, the judge will side with them.

Several days after the hearing, Jackie went by the apartment to see Margaret. She informed her that she believed that her word was true and that we would wait to collect the rent until after her benefits fiasco was cleared up. Margaret in turn told Jackie that she didn't have anything to worry about – that she would call just as soon as the check came in the mail.

How's this for a twist? About six days later, the phone rang. Margaret had the money. She was even kind enough to bring it over to us.

Jackie and I celebrated like the end of the world was nigh after we put that $2,500 in the bank.

Oh, reader, if only that were the resolution to the story. In effect, it was only the climax. There's plenty of grueling dénouement ahead.

The next morning, I received a call from a preacher asking if we had been paid. I told him we had. Evidently, this upset the preacher, as Margaret apparently owed him money, as well.

Collections Lesson #4: If your tenant owes you money, they probably owe other people money, too. Expect to claw and scratch with the other bill collectors.

Despite her clear financial woes, Margaret continued to rent from us for a couple more months. During this time, I was renovating the building next to hers, so I had plenty of opportunity to spy. I noticed that she had moved some guy in with her. In addition to that, a whole lot of trafficking seemed to be going on in the neighborhood – base of operations: Margaret's apartment. I didn't know exactly what she was up to, but I could guess. Drugs. Prostitution. Whatever it was, her customers sure seemed desperate.

Soon after, her name just seemed to keep cropping up in the arrest reports. Yep, prostitution. Fortunately for me and my sanity, the busts typically happened in one of the town's finer run-down hotels.

Despite her apparently booming business, Margaret started falling behind on the rent again. It got to the point where she was two months' behind. Between that and the arrest reports, Jackie and I finally came to our senses and decided to put a stop to this fiasco before it dragged on any further. Jackie drove to Margaret's apartment to have "the talk" with her, but as it turned out, she wasn't home. Fortune would favor us on that day, however, as Jackie would actually spot her from the car on her way back to our place. Margaret, it seemed, was spending her afternoons in the newly opened Bingo/Slot Machine business several blocks away.

Jackie parked her car in a nearby lot and waited for Margaret to get settled inside the gambling hall. She then strutted in and found Margaret sitting at a slot machine, a cigarette hanging casually out the side of her mouth.

"It's a shame you're putting all your rent money in the slots," Jackie said.

If Margaret was stunned to be confronted by her landlady, I'm told she didn't show it. She just kept playing the slots, an indifferent look on her face.

Jackie calmly informed our troublesome tenant that our business with her was over, asking her to vacate the apartment by the end of the month. To her credit, Margaret agreed to get out. She was out by the end of the month. She left owing money, but at least she was gone and spared us the aggravation of more court and extra costs.

The Ones You Least Expect

Here's a nice little cautionary tale about running the collections game. It takes place in what we'll call the Hunter Street House, which was a 4-bedroom place with 12-foot-high ceilings in a few of the rooms. Nice, right? Full disclosure: it also had rotten bathrooms, a major leak in the kitchen, and the additions to the house were not properly framed. I'll tell you all about the repairs later. For now, just know that it was a decent little house that took a whole hell of a lot of work to bring up to code.

One day after Hunter Street House was ready, Jackie picked up a call from a girl who needed a place to live. She had four children and was currently living in a house falling apart at the seams. Since she had a job and was in nursing school, she was okay with us.

Her name was Teri. She made enough money to pay the rent and she seemed like she was trying to get her life in order. The idea of a single mother going to nursing school was impressive to us, so we gave her the tour. She loved the house and we rented it to her immediately.

For a couple of months, Teri paid her rent on time and everything was going well. I would call to pick up the rent and she would leave it with one of her children. The children would occasionally invite me in to show off their new gear – like the new computer in the foyer, for example. In addition to these excellent signs, the house was always very neat and orderly.

But as things tend to go, as time went on, Teri started making later and later payments. She dropped out of school and was working at a job that barely allowed her to make ends meet. Then, she did the worst of the worst, as we all know: She moved a thug into the house. Joy of all joys, our regular arrests research turned up the name of her loving new thug. Domestic violence. We found out later that he was the direct source for her late rent payments (she'd used her rent money to bail this thug out of jail in the months she was late paying us).

Eventually, Teri got three months behind on the rent. But when I went to check on her, she was gone. She had even left her beautiful little gray and black spotted cocker spaniel tied to the front porch. I considered keeping it, but then decided it would be best to contact the humane society to come pick up the dog.

Collections Lesson #5: Dogs don't pay the bills.

I found out shortly that Teri had moved into the housing project. So we found her and sued her for damages and lost rent.

When the court date came, she was there with her children, claiming she didn't owe me for damages. "Someone must've come into the house after we left and done those damages," she said. With a straight face.

Fortunately, I had pictures and receipts to back up my side of the story. The judge awarded us $1,700.

Collections Lesson #6: Always take pictures for court. And bring receipts for repair work. The more, the better.

Teri really laid her lies on thick for the court audience and the judge. According to her, I never fixed things, it was always cold, the unit was horribly decrepit, and I had asked her repeatedly to stop seeing her boyfriend. The lies were so ridiculous and so embarrassing that I made a vow to myself right there in the courtroom that I wouldn't let Teri get away with welching on this debt, too. Wage garnishment, I thought, would be the answer.

Teri was working at the local Haley's Barbeque. Aside from the fact that it meant Jackie and I would no longer be able to eat there for fear of spit-on food, knowing Teri's current place of business would allow us to try to get the wage garnishment set in motion. But the manager at Haley's wrote a letter to the court on Teri's behalf. They couldn't garnish her wages because she only worked part time, see.

Collections Lesson #7: If you're dealing with low-income tenants, you're probably dealing with part-time workers. Forget about wage garnishment. It's useless.

I would find out later (through another tenant of mine who actually owned Haley's, no less), that Teri was getting preferential treatment at work in all senses of the word. The owner, see, had hired a charming little manager who took care of Teri. After I finally realized I had my back to the wall with Haley's and wasn't going to collect the money, I let it go.

But back to the owner of Haley's – a man from India named BJ. Of course, I never mentioned to him the business dealings I'd had with Teri, but I saw him at his apartment one day, exhausted. He told me he had to work long hours because he had to fire several employees. I dropped my arms to my side, relaxed, and listened carefully because it looked like he wanted to vent his frustration. I waited to hear Teri's name roll out of his mouth.

It did.

He revealed that, for months, he had been finding that food was missing and the cash receipts weren't adding up. So he gave a friend $15 to go into Haley's to buy sandwiches. Apparently, Teri and her son were working alone together the night this friend went in. They filled his order. He paid Teri in cash and left. Fifteen minutes later, BJ walked in and found that the cash receipts were missing and that there was no report that sandwiches had been sold. So he let Teri and her son go.

I just shook my head and told him I couldn't imagine how hard it must be to employ dishonest people. It was so hard for me to believe that this nice young mother who had once been in nursing school had devolved into a barbeque counter thief. And her poor kids. But I guess why go to school, get an education, and be a positive role model for your children when you can lie, cheat, and steal?

Oh well, not my problem anymore.

Insufficient Funds

Let's head on back to the Davis duplex, shall we? This next story occurs on the timeline right after our friend Billie Jean had to move out of 701B and good old Ms. Tallie had to vacate 701A.

Once 701B was back on the market, a couple walked up just as I was locking the door after my daily maintenance. They were looking for an apartment, so I opened the door and we went in. They liked it and said they wanted it immediately, so I gave them an application.

The woman, Carol, was the manager at Costella's Pizza. Her ambitious husband, Reverend Henry, worked at a building supply store with the hopes of becoming a policeman or fireman. Henry gave me a check for the security deposit and they agreed to sign the lease the following week. They would move in right after paying the first month's rent.

That all sounds great, right? Well, I wouldn't be telling you this story if we weren't talking about a collections issue, here. You guessed it, the check came back to me marked "INS," which of course means "Insufficient Funds." Get used to checks like these, reader.

So what did I do? I called Henry immediately. I distinctly remember his grand voice on the answering machine: "May the lord be upon you, etc., and have a blessed day."

The message I left went like this: "Rev, your check is bad."

When I didn't hear back from him, I decided to go directly to the building supply store where he worked to present him with the check.

Collections Lesson #8: Sometimes visiting your tenant's place of business is the only way to get what you want.

Well, the Reverend happily wrote me another check. Yep. It was bad, too. My next stop, then, was Costella's Pizza, where Carol cut me a check that actually cleared. From then on, she played sugar mama for the unit. She'd cover the rent each month.

We never accepted another payment from the Reverend, who must have been thoroughly enjoying his free ride. We still see this guy around town and laugh because he drives the nicest vehicles and always has a different one about every six months.

The Schemers

I'm not sure what it was about 807 Montgomery Street, but we always seemed to have our share of schemers in that place. Tenants there tended to play every angle they could to get out of paying rent.

As you'll recall from Chapter 2, 807 Montgomery Street was an old place with a big porch and an attached, rectangular storefront (which we had slowly converted into two one-bedroom efficiency apartments). Anyway, once I had finally gotten the apartments in the back of the house ready, we were set to search for a new tenant.

A little backstory for where we found her: Jackie had taken a job at a domestic violence shelter. It was there that she met a lady in need of an apartment. The lady (Thelma was her name) even had a job. Score.

Thelma was a good tenant for about three months.

Shortly after her move-in date, I began to notice that she spent a lot of time hanging out with some of the thugs from the neighborhood streets. One in particular was a tall skinny guy who was scarred severely, apparently from a savage burn. He didn't seem to have any other disability, but he was purportedly receiving a nice government check. Guess what? He moved in with Thelma. Guess what again? We never got another rent payment from her after that.

Bonus: Thelma also began complaining about the apartment for the first time. I would go over there, get the work done, and then leave as quickly as possible.

Meanwhile, Jackie and I were trying to collect the rent from her. One such collection day, Thelma pulled a new trick. One we'd never seen before. She matter-of-factly informed me that she had called the city engineer and that I was no longer allowed to collect rent on the apartment. Evidently, the disabled thug was from New York City (or some other northern city where landlords are required to have an occupancy authorization to collect rent on any given apartment). I guess it is common practice for tenants up there to damage their apartments and then call the city inspector out to revoke the certification. That way, they wouldn't have to pay the landlord any rent or back-rent. What a racket.

"This ain't New York City!" I told her. Then, I left. Next stop: the courthouse; where I filed for eviction, whistling all the while. On court day, the judge reminded Thelma that she had a month-to-month rental agreement and that she should have just moved out if she was unhappy with the conditions of the place.

"But you can't expect to stay for free," he said.

My heart leapt. We had her beat. He awarded us $1,600 for back rent and ordered her to get out.

Imagine this: I was never able to collect the money.

Collections Lesson #9: Court orders tend to mean next to squat to the kinds of people who owe back-rent. Don't count on any money, even if it's been awarded.

In short, reader, the court can give you a favorable judgment, but it's still next to impossible to collect. What usually happens is this: your low-income tenants are already typically working minimum wage jobs; the minute they see that their check has been cut due to a court order that has been applied, they quit that job and take another, causing you to have to re-file the wage garnishment. Pain. In. The. Ass. Sure, you can chase the deadbeat tenant around and pay the court to order their employer to garnish wages, but in the end you won't collect a penny. Anything you get will be spent on court ongoing fees.

So what we found is this: the court is really only useful in terms of eviction. After years of experience, Jackie and I have developed strategies to help us avoid the courts altogether – ways to motivate bad renters to get the hell out without the aid of a judge. More on those strategies later.

Another common scheme amongst low-income tenants is a scheme on the government itself. Many will claim disability when there is no real disability at issue. This entitles them to a monthly check, which they occasionally use to pay their rent (occasionally).

In our rural Alabama town, a very large percentage of the population draws SSI for disability. One day, we had just such a woman – a charming older woman – apply for one of our apartments. Jackie did a background check and income verification and found that we had ourselves a decent little tenant.

As far as cleanliness goes, she would turn out to be exactly that. In fact, she was so cleanly that on the day she signed her new lease; she drove up in her new car and requested that I do something to remove the black mildew in front of her door. She leaned over the driver side window to tell me she might have an accident, slipping on the mildew, because of her disability. I must have looked at her funny because she looked me in the eye and said, "Oh, I'm blind." She then pulled off and merged into traffic on Highway 80. For a blind person, she was the best driver I've ever seen. She didn't work, either, which gave her plenty of time to run the roads – seemingly her favorite hobby.

Now that I'm thinking about it, I remember that after moving into the apartment, she wanted the living room painted because she couldn't stand looking at the color. Looking. She would give us the whole sad story about being disabled and then jump into her car and speed away.

Disability. We had another couple apply for an apartment and found they had over $4,000 a month in disability checks coming to them. We wouldn't rent to them because of past credit issues – after all, since they were on disability, if they eventually chose not to pay us, we wouldn't be able to garnish their wages. But in any case, the husband and wife team were both on disability. The husband drove a brand new 4-door, duel-axle monster truck. Almost every day, you could see him at the gas station loading a cooler with ice and beer for his golf game. I've heard he's a pretty good golfer.

Getting "Hands-On" with Collections

Anna Trueman was a thin, attractive, polite, and single mother of three. Cute kids, too. Her son Timmy had a million dollar smile and always had endless questions for me whenever I worked on a project near Anna's apartment. This would all have been good and well except for the fact that his mother always had trouble with her rent. So I'd always have to go over and collect.

Jackie would usually call ahead to Anna to find out when she was going to have the rent. One month, Anna told Jackie to come by on a Thursday morning at ten. Jackie did as she was asked; loading up our twins and driving to Anna's mid-morning (it was summer, so the kids weren't in school). Anyway, my wife knocked on the door and Anna's adorable son Adrian answered. He told Jackie that the mail hadn't run yet. When Jackie protested, Anna came to the door and explained that her paycheck had not yet arrived and that she couldn't pay until it did.

Collections Lesson #10: Get to know the mail routes in your tenants' neighborhoods.

Well, Jackie had followed Lesson #10. She knew the mail route in Anna's neighborhood. So she told Anna that she would be back at 1pm to collect. "That should give you enough time to get to the bank, too," she said.

When Jackie returned, she got another sob story from Anna. She finally had her paycheck, it seemed, but no ride to the bank. Well, Jackie wasn't having any of that nonsense. She waved her hand and demanded that a wide-eyed Anna get in her car. My wife would be driving her to the bank herself.

"But I'm not dressed," Anna pleaded. "And I don't have anyone to watch the kids."

"I can wait," Jackie said. "And you can bring your kids along." The bank was just around the corner, so my wife figured that they could rough it with two women and five kids in one compact car. Jackie then went to the car and told our boys to scoot over. "It's gonna be a little tight, guys."

After waiting for a while for Anna to get dressed and ready, Jackie was able to throw the car into gear and drive the whole crew over to the bank, where they pulled up to the drive-through window. Imagine the clerk's face to see all those children in one car.

Anyway, here's how hands-on Jackie was on that day: Anna endorsed her check and handed it over to the teller; the teller completed the transaction and put it in the container; then Jackie opened the container and took out $250 for the rent, handing Anna the rest.

My wife was of course cordial during this whole operation, thanking Anna for her patience and explaining that we had to be sure to collect the rent or we wouldn't be able to pay our mortgage. She then drove everyone home and helped Anna get the kids out of the car. She finished up by giving our perplexed tenant a receipt and telling her to have a great day.

Let's finish up our chapter with the Walnut Street apartments – which you'll recall from Chapter One as being a series of five duplexes residing across the street from the Panty Fair factory. This was the place that gave us the least amount of trouble at first, as most of the tenants we inherited actually paid their rent (though it was rarely on time). *Most* of the tenants we inherited...

Jackie decided it was time that we took this late-rent issue into our own hands. So she started giving our tenants a little incentive to pay on time. To that end, she offered a prize drawing for tenants who paid their rent in full by the

5th of the month. What a concept. I thought it was genius. We gave away a crock-pot, a coffee pot, and dishes before we realized that most of our tenants actually *wanted* to pay, but found difficulty in coming up with the full amount of rent by the 5th. So our bubble quickly burst. This property soon became a challenge in the rent department, but it was a challenge that Jackie proved up for – clocking in at 100% on rent collection each month. I was amazed sometimes when she would come home and tell me that she had gotten so-and-so's rent.

But I can only give such glowing reviews if I ignore one particular unit at Walnut Street. One lady named Christy hadn't paid her rent to the previous owner in over a year – and we'd been warned that she might be difficult. I guess the previous owner harbored a soft spot for Christy or something (which was easy to do, given that she had seven children to care for). Anyway, the eight of them were living in a three-bedroom apartment for only $185 per month. Or I guess it was for $0 per month, in her case.

When we bought the property, it was in need of a great deal of repair, so I worked on Christy's unit first. It boasted significant leaks in the kitchen and bathroom. The leaks had led to the bathroom floor becoming so rotten that the only thing holding it up was the pipe for the toilet. All over the unit, there were spots in the sheetrock that had been broken, probably from an abusive boyfriend or the children running around and crashing into things. Every time I would enter her apartment to make repairs, Christy would claim that the damage had been there when she first arrived. After a couple of years of continuous repairs, I finally asked her to please quit saying that because I had fixed the same walls three or four times.

She laughed.

But during my first few visits, I began by fixing the bathroom. I pulled her toilet and cut the pipe below the floor decking. I taped together newspaper and made a size pattern of the floor. I taped the pattern on a piece of ¾ inch of plywood and cut the flooring to perfect size. I then carried the piece inside and covered the entire space of flooring, including the old tiles. Screwed the plywood down, I then reinstalled a toilet flange using a new kind of flexible rubber connection sleeve. It took me about an hour before Ms. Christy had a safe and functional bathroom once again.

Despite all this goodwill flying around, Jackie still had to make several trips to Christy's apartment to collect the rent. One day, Christy met her at the door and told her she didn't have it. They went inside and sat down. Jackie explained that we needed the money to pay our mortgage – that if Christy didn't pay, we'd be forced to evict her.

"Then where would you live?" Jackie asked. "The housing project?"

Well, that did the trick. Christy cried and told Jackie that she had lived in the projects before and never wanted to go back. So the two of them worked out a plan – Jackie even helped Christy create a budget, explaining that shelter should be the top priority on that budget – to prevent Christy's children from having to grow up in such a harsh and dangerous environment.

Meanwhile, Christy was always calling with repair requests. Given the dual nature of our dealings – my constant repairs and Jackie's constant collection efforts – I made sure to schedule the repairs around the 3rd (coincidentally, the day when her check from the government would arrive in the mail). It was the check Christy received for having a mentally handicapped son that would allow her to pay the rent.

Some months later, Christy finally got a job at the nursing home. And I will say that she wore her uniform proudly. She was a hard worker, but unfortunately went through a slew of loser boyfriends. Eventually, though, she got married to a decent guy. And thanks to Jackie's help with her budget, she stayed current on her rent for over ten years. We really liked Christy and her kids, so that was cool with us.

But not all was right in paradise. One day, I was working on the duplex next to Christy's when I noticed several people pulling up to her unit in a black sedan. I just figured it was DHR (it's not unusual to see social services in low-income areas). Man was I wrong. I had a guy working for me on the property adjacent – doing some repairs on the cheap – and he told me that the men in the sedan were from an outfit with a much different acronym: DEA. Word had it that drugs were being sold from Christy's unit.

I was flabbergasted. Jackie and I immediately thought this was a new activity since her marriage. We knew she had some real losers as boyfriends, but it was amazing to us that she would be wrapped up in something like that, especially considering how sweet her kids were, always smiling and looking after their handicapped brother.

I had been thinking about converting the 3-bedroom duplex into a home for a large family, maybe a woman with children who wanted to return to college for a nursing or teaching career. Well, this suspicious activity convinced us to convert the unit, so Jackie helped Christy find a nicer place to live (read "a *different* place to live"). She didn't want to leave at first and asked to stay. This had been their home for so many years, after all. But I told her it was time to renovate the worn out apartment.

So the final lesson here is that no matter who your tenants are, no matter what schemes they may pull, sometimes all they need is a little help. The court can order them to pay you, but in the end, they won't pay anyway. Show them that you are willing to work with them, willing to come to their aid if need be, and they will respect you all the more for it. And respect, reader, tends to lead to a regular check.

Chapter Five

You know what the fun part about Davis 701A and 701B was? The freewheeling tenants? Well, yeah, that was kind of fun. Funny, anyway. The constant complaints? No. That's never fun. The fact that we always seemed to be begging tenants for our rent money and taking them to collections? C'mon, reader. I'd rather have an enema.

No, the most fun part about Davis 701A and 701B was the fact that, every time we kicked a tenant out of the units, we would have wall to wall repairs to look forward to. As you will learn from this chapter – and this opening story about the Davis Duplex – repairing and renovating apartment units (particularly of the low-income variety) takes one hell of a lot of work, and often, more money than you'll care to think about.

So let's get back to our story. There was a time when 701A and B were both vacant. And, oh, what a mess. Step one for me: change the locks. Actually, let's call that lesson #1.

Repairs and Renovations Lesson #1: Your first step should always be to change the locks. You never know which of your old tenants might want to show up and steal things, squat for a night or two, or inflict more damage on the work you've already completed. Bitter former tenants are funny that way...

In any case, once I had installed new locks and could turn my attention to the rest of these two apartments, I was pretty well flabbergasted. How two people could inflict so much damage on two apartments was beyond me. Long story short, we would need some help on this one. With so many repairs needed, there was just no way I'd be able to go it alone.

Rusty and Beth Davis to the rescue! At one point, Jackie had been looking for someone to help us with the cleaning of one of our other units – and it was then that she had met Ms. Beth. She cleaned up a company called Wood Appliance every afternoon while her husband, Rusty cut grass. They were an older couple, but they were still up for the occasional bout with heavy lifting. So Jackie and I put them to work on hauling off all the trash and debris from the two vacant apartments. The whole process took us several days. Yeah…there was that much trash.

Ms. Beth would pick through the refuse for anything that she deemed of value. Then, she would ask me if she could keep it. I would just shrug my shoulders and say, "Sure." Old Beth always seemed to know someone who could use whatever piece of junk she was holding.

Having already reached my wits end on low-income scammers, I was determined to use this opportunity for renovation to fix up the apartments nice enough to attract a higher level of tenant. But the first question was, how do I tackle these two large projects? Do I renovate them both simultaneously or do I do one at a time? I chose the latter. This proved to be a good idea because, once 701B was finished (I started with B because it wasn't quite as poor off as A, at the time), I could use it as my storage area for all the heavy tools I would need for 701A. It proved to be a bad idea for several other reasons…

More good news came when Jackie started receiving calls regarding the ad we had placed in the newspaper. Seeing as how these callers actually spent time reading the paper, my wife and I assumed that we could look forward to slightly more educated future tenants. At least we knew these tenants could read (incidentally, most of our previous tenants had found us by stumbling up and seeing our "For Rent" signs from the sidewalk). Our first educated caller would meet with us on the coming Friday afternoon.

701B – the one the caller was interested in inspecting – looked very nice once renovations were complete. So nice, in fact, that we were actually going to be proud to show it. Feeling like I'd just need one last once-over of the unit, I went back to examine my work and collect my tools.

I opened the door to 701B and immediately realized that I would not be collecting my tools. Why? They were missing. Stolen. More great news: whoever had broken in to take my things had also been kind enough to tag the walls of 701B with loads of graffiti.

Repairs and Renovations Lesson #2: When dealing with low-income housing, sometimes changing the locks still isn't enough. If you have pissed off ex-tenants, plan on (and budget for) doing some of your work twice.

Even though it was a huge headache, it was fortunately only paint that I was dealing with here. I've had walls kicked in, windows knocked out, ceiling fans torn down, you name it. In this case, all I had to do was go next door to 701A, grab up some of the extra heavy duty white paint I had waiting over there, and make the apartment presentable once more. Graffiti problem solved.

Next problem: how did the graffiti get there in the first place? I had changed the locks. None of the windows or doors had been broken or kicked in. How did my unknown little graffiti artists manage to get inside? Then, it hit me like a ton of bricks. They entered through 701A, got up into the attic, and then shimmied over to the other side. A quick scan of 701A confirmed my suspicions. They'd broken a window over there.

155

Now that I had riddled them out, I knew there were two things I could do. I could either a) replace the window and wait for the thugs to break it again or b) install a set of cameras to catch the punks in the act. I went with option "b." This entailed installing cameras in both 701A and 701B and hiding them behind a standard smoke detector cover. I also stashed a camera on the back porch (near the broken window) under a pile of old clothes and trash. There. All my bases were covered. The only issue was that I had to run wires to the cameras – but I figured my intruders would be too amped up to notice anything like that; plus, they would be attacking at night, no doubt.

That night, Jackie and our two boys cooked out on the grill. I thought about all the evidence I was collecting as Jackie and I sipped our beers and evaluated the applications for 701B. It was a nice evening.

The next day, I returned to the duplex to collect my evidence, but instead discovered that the thieves had not only stolen the rest of my tools, but also the security system! Well, hell. That was it. I'd had it. So I called the police and completed an incident report. Let me tell you, reader, the detective was rolling with laughter as I described what had happened.

Later, I told Jackie about what had happened. Our boys were apparently listening in, because I could hear them giggling in the background. After allowing me to bark at them for a minute, Jackie went to the refrigerator and returned with two bottles of Bud Light. She popped the top and handed me one.

"Thank goodness for Bud Light," she said, touching the neck of her bottle to mine.

I grinned, sighed, and took a sip.

The next morning, we received a call from the detective I'd filed my report with. He had located some of my equipment at an apartment in the housing projects. Unfortunately, I couldn't come up with all the serial numbers I needed, so the detective was unable to make a case to recover the property.

I guess the thieves realized that a report had been made and that the police were on to them, because they never returned to the property. I had my suspects in mind, though: not least among them being Billie Jean's wayward son, the aggressive little thug in training, former resident of 701B.

The Overhauls

Jackie and I owned a unit that has had a great history of tenants but a spotty history of repairs and renovations. When we first bought the place, we would get our share of jerks and losers, true, but once it was finally fixed up completely, we would wind up with a nice long string of school teachers and professionals. But it was a long hard road to this point...

I remember our first tenant in the unit after it was renovated the first time. Remember that I said "first time," as that's important to the story. We'll call the tenant Rose. Rose was a sweet woman who worked at the Panty Fair factory across the street – a factory that, incidentally, had to close a mere three months after NAFTA was passed; but

I won't get into all that political garbage. Let me just say this before I move on: The administration at Panty Fair had actually come to the city council asking for everyone to support the trade agreement, claiming that it would definitely not affect the local plant. No Shit.

Despite the promises from the suits, within a year, our plant and most of the other plants in the surrounding area were closed. Rose, meanwhile, quietly remained in her apartment quietly for a couple of years until she could no longer afford it and had to move into the new housing projects. We hated to see her move, but money was just too tight for her to manage. She was always a great tenant who took care of the property, even keeping the yard beautiful with flowers, elephant ears, and other plants. We would miss her dearly.

Particularly when her successors moved in...

Our first mistake was trusting Margaret Price/Lawson with a referral. Our old friend Margaret (this was prior to our long strange collections nightmare, by the way) gave me the name of a couple who had children and needed a place to live. The names? Katy and Leo Mason. Both of them received government checks, which at the very least means guaranteed money every month (assuming they use that money to pay the rent, of course).

It would only take Katy and Leo eight months to completely destroy our newly renovated unit.

One day, I was working on the sewer line (the Masons had been complaining for weeks about issues with their plumbing). Despite Leo's documented disability, he wanted to help me with the work. The old line, I found, was over 300 feet long. All asphalt, this pipe. Asphalt that was broken and collapsed in spots. A leak had formed and sewage was running into the ditch. Nasty.

I would need to be clever on this particular job, as I couldn't afford a backhoe (a kind of tractor with a shovel). So I rented its much cheaper cousin, a trencher (a machine that digs four to six inch wide ditches. The problem with this arrangement is that the work requires that you angle the pipe within the ditch to facilitate drainage. With my narrow trench (6 inches) and inadequate tools, this was no easy task. The fact that I was replacing the asphalt pipe with plastic certainly helped, but still…

So with Leo's hand and a rope, I lowered the whole thing into the ditch. I tied the ropes to sticks, and the whole rigging held the pipe aloft. This way, by twisting the sticks, I could raise or lower the pipe within the narrow space. Now all I needed to do was figure out the proper angle.

What I did was I taped a small stack of coins to one end of my level. Then, I eyeballed the pipe, lowering it down to what I figured was the correct angle. And finally, I set the level on top of the plastic and measured it out. After some tweaking, I eventually got it right.

Satisfied with myself, I made sure to support the pipe from beneath with fresh dirt. The last step was to bury it all up once more.

Anyway, I hope I haven't lost you on all this sewage detail. The main thing to glean from this story is that, if you hired a professional, a typical sewer job of this nature would cost somewhere between $30,000 and $40,000. Imagine what that would do to one's cash flow. Instead, I took the initiative and did the whole project for under $600. Call it sweat equity.

Unfortunately, this wouldn't be the last time I would get toilet complaints from old Leo. Incidentally, the first time I went into his apartment to handle the complaint, I noticed he was painting the rooms. I mean, he had blood red paint on one wall about halfway up – definitely not finished. One section of another wall was green. I wasn't too worried about the paint because I was familiar with sheetrock repair and knew I could handle it when they moved out. But still, you should understand that your tenants are probably going to do whatever the hell they want with the walls, regardless of what you tell them.

Rather than screwing around, I decided to replace Leo's toilet with a new model. When I was finished with the swap, I discovered a toy car had been lodged in the old toilet. Oh well. New toilet, new sewer line, I was finished for the day.

A couple of days later, I was working on another unit when Leo came up to me with a big grin on his fat face. He asked me if I could come back again to look at his toilet. Again. I sighed and walked behind him to his bathroom. When he opened the door, I almost vomited.

In the corner of the room was a bucketful of shit and piss. Holding my breath, I mumbled, "Are you *saving* that or something?"

Leo shook his dumbass head and took the bucket out to the back yard, where he dumped it. Catching my breath, I leaned down to unplug the new toilet. I had no luck with an auger, so I stuck a water hose into the bottom under the base. Shortly, I could hear the hose filling up.

Suddenly, a huge pile of tan-colored shit started oozing up, all blob-like. Horrified, I thought it was going to explode. It rolled out slowly. It was all I could do to hold down my lunch. Thoroughly disgusted, I watched as the shit blob was followed by a disposable douche bottle. That was it. I turned my head and started throwing up. Leo laughed his ass off as I puked.

One of Leo's babies stood behind me as I wiped my mouth. As I walked away, I noticed that he had about fifty blow flies stuck to his shit-filled diaper, which was leaking putrid green fluid. For a moment, the ground started to spin again. Leo apparently thought it was the funniest thing he had ever seen. I remember Jackie driving up just as I had finished getting sick. I asked her to bring me a drink.

Somehow, I managed to reinstall the toilet. While I worked, Leo's woman, Katy, was screaming at the babies. It sounded hellish. So I asked Leo to go help her, hoping it would make the screaming stop.

When I finished the work, I was able to take some time to look around. Busted walls. Paint spills and splatters everywhere. And get this: they had put a padlock on one of the bedroom doors. A quick listen told me that Leo and Katy had locked their kids within. Man, I bet when those kids are old enough to talk, their first words will be "mother" and "fuckers."

I contacted social services about the babies being locked in the bedroom – to say nothing of the general state of the apartment. As I learned from SS, Leo's name was not actually Leo Mason. It was Leon Jarvis. Here's why he'd given me a false name: Leon Jarvis had a reputation for destroying homes and apartments. We'd been beaten at our own rental game. The non-existent Leo Mason didn't have a record of eviction when we checked the court records...

Furious, I went back and demanded that Leon and company leave the apartment. Social Services, meanwhile, informed Mr. Jarvis that if he didn't get a bigger apartment by the following month, they would take his children. I can't imagine how they let them keep those babies for five more minutes, let alone thirty more days.

In any case, the Mason/Jarvis family moved out. But still, I can't help but feel bad. His mere existence is a tremendous indictment on the scorecard of Alabama Social Services. The story has a happy ending, though. I would find out some months later that those poor babies were eventually taken under the wing of the state.

The...Opportunities

The building we owned next door to the Mason/Jarvis family was another duplex, rented on one side to Walter Nice and on the other to Anna Trueman. You remember Anna Trueman, of course – the one my wife had to drive to the bank herself. Well, prior to my wife getting a little more "hands on" with collections, Anna spent plenty of time being a bit of a hassle on the rent front. At first, it was my job to collect the rent. That didn't last...

Here's why:

One thing you should know about going into people's houses to make repairs, they sometimes use the opportunity to barter for lower rent, if you catch my drift. During my time repairing apartments, I've been offered any number of valuable things in lieu of payment, but none more embarrassing than what Anna seemed to be offering.

See, one day, when I knocked on her door to collect the rent, she answered it in a nightgown. A half-opened nightgown. At first, I thought it was just a one-time accidental thing. Like maybe she forgot that she wasn't wearing much of anything. But then it started to happen every time I dropped by to make fixes. The look in her eye always suggested that she was hoping to make a trade. I ran this by Jackie and the two of us decided that it'd be a good idea if my wife went to pick up the checks from then on.

Anna always seemed to try to be a good tenant. And she was certainly appreciative whenever we fixed things in her apartment. That's not unusual, though. I mean, if your toiled hadn't flushed properly in months, you'd appreciate the guy who came in to fix it for free, right? Of course you would. But Anna and her children weren't long for our place. Eventually, they had to get an apartment in the housing projects. Anna never had a job, so one can only guess how she came up with the money for the months that she did. She owed us about two months' rent when she left, but that didn't seem worth chasing after, considering some of the other tenants we had encountered.

I did the best I could for those units, but the low rent we were charging sometimes made the logistics difficult. It's tough to afford $200 jobs when you only charge $165 a month. So over time, our units weren't exactly beautiful, but at least everything worked.

In my life, I've had the curse of being average in everything, except when it comes to fixing things. I was trained as a little boy to take a bathroom valve apart and fix it properly using washers and graphite. For two or three dollars, I can repair a fixture that would normally cost $100 to replace.

But enough about my handyman prowess. Let's talk about Walter Nice.

Walter, true to his name, was a nice tenant. He worked the same job for ten years and always paid his rent on time. I could always count on finding a check for me in his mailbox whenever I swung by to pick up the rent. Plus, he lived alone and never caused any trouble. A dream tenant, right?

Only problem was that dream tenants, in neighborhoods such as these, tend to get picked on. The pack can sense the weak amongst the heard. So naturally, it was only a matter of time before this nice guy started having thugs target him for burglary. During Walter's time in our unit, he was broken into four times. Four! Poor guy even had the cops stealing from him. For the first break-in, during the investigation, the police seized a trunk full of Walter's CDs, claiming they were illegal. Walter protested – claiming that he had bought them from the annual foot washing festival in a rural part of Hale County – but it was to no avail.

So why am I telling this story? Simple. It imparts a lesson.

Repairs and Renovations Lesson #3: Your tenants will have break-ins. Treat them like opportunities to upgrade their apartments.

In the case of Walter Nice, I was the master of Lesson #3. Every time he was broken into, I would rush over to fix the place up. It was nice to have these opportunities to make improvements, but I felt so bad for Walter. I mean, why didn't he just move? He just didn't seem all that concerned about it. Polite and nice guys always finish last, I guess.

Now Walter shared a wall with Anna, but he also shared a wall with a woman named Winnie. There wasn't anything wrong with Winnie, necessarily, except that she kept thuggish friends. One day, a group from Winnie's apartment kicked a hole in the wall she shared with Walter. They entered Walter's place and stole a big bottle of spare change. I would later find out that the group included a kid named Tawuna Corpus and the infamous Shawn Lawson. The two geniuses were caught because they only got two blocks to Food World before temptation to turn the change into cash got the better of them. The manager at Food World became suspicious and called the cops.

When I got word of the incident, I plowed over to the unit and repaired the wall, putting plywood on the inside to prevent the problem from occurring again. See? Upgrades.

Somehow, Walter managed to remain neighbors with Winnie until we got so fed up with her that we had to tell her to get out. Our problems didn't end there, however.

After her apartment was vacant, someone climbed through her window, kicked a hole in the wall again and robbed Walter. Fortunately for us, the dumbass who did it dropped his wallet. The offending party? Shawn Lawson. Right there in black and white. The best part was that the license actually said that Shawn was now 18. So I was delighted to know that he would go to prison this time.

Once I took care of Lawson down at the police station, I was free to gut Winnie's unit. After installing new ceiling, flooring, and appliances, the place looked great – great enough to raise the rent $125.00 per month; great enough to rent it to a nice couple for a change (which we did within a few days of putting it up on the market).

So that's the takeaway message for Chapter Four, reader. Repairs and renovations may be difficult – and you may find that all your hard work only winds up getting damaged again by tenants or just plain bad luck – but in the end, they are almost always worth it. The nicer you keep your places, the nicer will be your tenants (for the most part). And even if you do continue to run into the shitty tenant once in a while, at least you'll know that the rent money is better than it used to be. Keep the faith and repairs and renovations will eventually pay for themselves in spades.

Chapter Six

Flipping Houses and Apartments

If I may, I'd like to spark this chapter about the money that can be made (and troubles that can be had) in flipping houses and apartments by getting back to the Hunter House. Long story short, Jackie and I were both pretty well sick of this old house after two years of constant trouble. As if in answer to our prayers, one day while I was working on the place, a young lady (we'll call her Carol) approached me and asked to see the house. I readily agreed.

She fell in love with it immediately, practically begging me to allow her to buy it. Apparently, Carol had a job tending to a wealthy elderly woman, so I guess she had the cash to jump feet first into the glamorous world of homeownership. I told her I'd be willing to part with the place for $15,000, which seemed like a reasonable price to me.

Carol's return figure was a little disappointing, as it was 20% lower than what I had in mind.

Flipping Houses and Apartments Lesson #1: Don't like negotiating? Get used to it, reader. It just comes with the territory.

Carol had apparently gone to her banker and discovered that she could only get access to $12,000. Normally, I'd have figured that this was just a negotiating tactic, a scam to set us up for agreeing to a number way under value. But Carol seemed sincere enough. At the very least, her "overwhelmingly disappointed" act played pretty well on my heart strings.

Exhausted of my patience with Hunter House, I let my guard down and agreed to the $12,000.

Flipping Houses and Apartments Lesson #2: You're never going to get exactly the figure you quote. That's just part of the negotiating process. And if you've had it with a house or apartment, be ready to take far less than you would have liked.

So we closed the deal at a banker's office in Linden. We were happy to be done with it. The house was just too large for a rental property, I guess. Plus, Jackie and I found that it attracted large poor families who would literally consume the property and then skip out. Regardless, cash in hand, Jackie and I had reason to celebrate once again.

But you have to understand that just because I tell this story first, that doesn't mean it was our first property sale. In truth, the process of reaching a critical mass of cash flow that could support us took several years – and overlapped with the ownership of other properties that I have yet to discuss. Still, by the time we sold Hunter House, we were one amazed married couple. Even with all these mortgages and repairs to deal with, we still had never had so much cash! No Money Down Millions really, *really* works, reader. You just have to be willing to take your lumps.

Before we settled into the real estate business, Jackie and I would have maybe $200 left over from our salaried jobs at the end of each month. Now, even in these relatively early stages, we would have $2,000 or more. It didn't necessarily feel like it at the time, but we were accumulating wealth. Rapidly.

I remember the day we bought new vehicles. When Jackie and I started our real estate adventure, we had a red, two-door Geo Metro with great gas mileage. This was nice because about every other day, we were on the road to Meridian or Tuscaloosa to shop at Lowe's for maintenance supplies. The local building supply store was just too expensive for us. We would pile all our supplies in that tiny car and Jackie would sit on the passenger's side with vinyl siding draped across her lap and jutting out the window.

I would crank the car up, look at her, and smile. "You ok?" I would ask.

She would smile and instruct me to turn the music up and drive to the liquor store for a six-pack.

And we would live like this for a long time, carting to and fro from the supply store in a car grossly unequipped for the hauling we were doing. But by the time we collected on Hunter House, we had enough scratch to move up to the next level. We were happy as we made our way home, as I recall. We knew our bills would be paid and our children would be cared for and happy. Life was great.

It didn't take me long to sort out why life was great at that particular moment, either. We had just sold a house. This meant a whole hell of a lot of cash flow. The answer, naturally, would be to sell more houses. Maybe even buy more houses, renovate them, and sell them for a higher price.

If only I'd known what I was getting into.

The Phony Buyers

You remember Eunice from 807 Montgomery Street, I'm sure. Hers was a sordid history with us. But let me tell you her role in our flipping houses and apartments initiative. To tell this story properly, we have to go back to the roots of good Eunice...

It was a hot day, I remember, when a lady from Chicago showed up to 807 Montgomery Street, looking for an apartment for her daughter, Eunice. I was working on renovating the store space, remember, so this lady was able to walk up to me and start her inquiry into the monthly rent. As I learned that day, Eunice was at the time living in the country with her aunt, but wanted to be in town, closer to where she worked. We would later meet Eunice and learn that she had a small child – and, more importantly, received her paychecks on the first of every month.

Well, Eunice's mother was able to set up Eunice's aunt as the payee. We were told by all three women involved that we would have no trouble collecting the rent. The number we agreed upon was $175 per month.

As we quickly discovered, sometimes Jackie and I would be forced to ride out to Eunice's aunt's house to collect the rent. She just couldn't be trusted to mail it in. It was a hassle, at times, but that one rent check paid the mortgage, tax, and insurance on the property, so we were willing to go the extra mile.

Let's talk about Eunice. She was short and chubby and pleasant. Man, she loved to talk. She had been in an accident that left a severe scar on her arm and torso, but apart from that, she was mobile and busy. The main problem with Eunice was that she seemed to be a lost child looking for love.

Eunice's apartment was on a corner that featured a lot of heavy walking traffic, even for that neighborhood. The school was about a block away, see. Old Eunice loved to sit on her front doorstep and watch the traffic and take in all that went on around her. On occasion, she would serve as our thug alarm. She would call us at all hours of the night, informing us of thuggish activity on or around that busy corner.

Well, the man living in the property on the corner opposite Eunice was a gentleman named Abraham. I use the term "gentleman" lightly here, bear in mind. Anyway, Eunice was always barking about a guy named Abraham, which was a coincidence, given that Abraham, actually a tenant of ours, was always barking to us about what a shithole he lived in. He was an especially vocal and arrogant guy, that Abraham. A man in his forties, he had recently moved back home from a large city to be closer to his mother. Joy of joys, he had chosen to live in one of our places.

The wrap on Abraham was that he had opened a Moslem Book store. In our little town. Yeah, that lasted about six months. So I guess with his newfound free time, he decided it would be best to constantly call and complain. After several such calls, he suggested that I just give the property to his sister, a woman he assured me would be a proper buyer. I told him that I would sell it to her for $25,000. I was such a sucker that I actually met his sister and showed her the property. She couldn't afford it.

One Fourth of July – and remember this date, reader, as it tends to bring the freaks out of the woodwork – Jackie answered the telephone. It was Abraham, talking about a relative in town who wanted to look at the house we were trying to sell. Gullibly, Jackie and I loaded up the boys and went to show the property.

The buyers looked it over, but couldn't decide. Bummer. They would never get back to us. And that house would sit on the market for an entire year.

The next Fourth of July, Abraham called with another relative. Jackie and I would laugh because every Fourth of July, Abraham would call with a buyer.

Flipping Houses and Apartments Lesson #3: Houses don't always sell right away. Expect at least a few of them to sit on the market for weeks, months, and even years at a time.

On one call, Abraham was sure he had a buyer. Unable to curb my curiosity, I went to meet the guy. He was a big black guy from Chicago. I'm not even kidding, he was wearing a ten-gallon cowboy hat. He shook my hand and gave me a bright, charming smile. He started right away with his plans for the house. He had a good line, this guy. I remember thinking that Abraham was right this time. *This* was the buyer.

This scene has left an indelible image on my brain:

Abraham's latest friend shook my hand and said, "Let me give you my business card. I'll be in touch." Then, he reached into his pocket for his wallet. When he opened up the wallet, a whole pile of business cards fell out.

I was quicker than he was, darting down to scoop up a few of them from the sidewalk. They were all different, these cards, but they bore one distinct similarity: they all carried the buyer's name. His supposed professions ranged from real estate to auto repair to handyman to loan officer. The one he finally handed me suggested that he was involved with some kind of long distance service.

I feigned a smile and waved him off. As he was leaving, I took a looked at the Cadillac he was driving. A rental. I guess he must have headed back to Chicago because we never heard from him again. That was the story with

Abraham's friends and relatives. They all drove Cadillacs, talked a big game, and then never came back.

Flipping Houses and Apartments Lesson #4: Most buyers (particularly of low-income houses) talk a big game. Few actually have the checking accounts to back it up.

That night I'd shown the place to my last phony buyer, I decided that the neighborhood had defeated me. So I decided to cash in my chips and *really* work to sell Abraham's place. The problem with this property was that I had paid very little for it. Adding insult to injury, I had failed to do a thorough inspection of the house prior to buying.

Flipping Houses and Apartments Lesson #5: *Always* do a thorough inspection of the house prior to buying.

Having not followed Lesson #5, I was in for huge disappointment once I kicked Abraham out and started work on renovating the place. I discovered that the rear apartment – the one Abraham had been in – had been added after a fire. The front of the house had trusses that had been pretty thoroughly charred. Given the severe damage, I would need to replace it all in order for the house to appreciate in value.

At the time, I didn't have enough experience or help to complete that task. I mean, repairing structural fire damage is a hell of a lot of work. So I just cleaned up the property and put out the "For Sale" sign.

I must say, despite my half-assed efforts, the house looked beautiful. We had replaced all the flooring, painted the place inside and out, and put up a new roof. The neighbors were excited and several made comments on how pretty the place was looking.

Long story short, once we had put in the effort to renovate, we finally got a buyer who wasn't a total phony. In fact, he was a funeral home owner, and he came by to tell us that he was interested in buying the house. We sold it to him for $38,000. After mortgage and fees, Jackie and I took home $14,000 in cash!

This property was a real hassle, but looking back I learned many lessons. For one thing, Jackie never wanted to buy it in the first place. And let me tell you, reader, if you are a man and you are married, listen to your wife. If your wife doesn't want it, don't buy it. Women tend to have greater intuition on things like these. Also, before buying anything, you really need to step back and look at the neighborhood. Think about this question: Who is going to rent this property? Is it going to be a trustworthy professional with a regular paycheck or someone with bad credit and a bad job?

I've flipped houses for a long time. So I've seen neighborhoods turn around during real estate booms. But more often than not, you won't be able to beat a neighborhood and its history. Police and detectives can't clean up an entire city block, much less six of them. If the neighborhood in which you've chosen to purchase a property isn't populated by good, decent people, you can't possibly expect to sell to a good, decent person.

Anyway, after that sale, Jackie and I had another celebration. From that point onward, our evenings got quieter and our skills grew stronger.

Lord of the Roaches

I hope you don't have a weak constitution, reader, because telling this story makes even my skin crawl.

Let's return to Walter Nice. Even though he was a great (though unfortunate) tenant, he apparently wasn't a particularly cleanly one. Or maybe it was my own fault. Who knows? See, after Walter moved out, I left the apartment empty for a couple of weeks before starting renovation. By the time I finally went to work on it, I saw immediately that I had a serious problem. It was roach infested. Terribly roach infested.

Flipping Houses and Apartments Lesson #6: Don't like bugs? Get used to them.

I remember when I first met Jackie she would scream at the sight of a roach. Her career as a landlord quickly got her over the fear. She had learned Lesson #6. But in this case, when I say terrible infestation, I mean terrible infestation. There were so many roaches in Walter's old apartment that it took me at least three weeks to kill them all. I sprayed a mixture of the strongest poisons I could find, then sprayed again in the hopes of getting the juvenile roaches before they matured and started reproducing.

But as with any bug problems – particularly roach problems – I got a little concerned about what was going on behind the walls. The couple now living next door to the place might find a little more concern, even. See, when I was doing my spray-work, I saw a scrum of roaches fleeing into the next door unit. The couple next door never complained, but I treated their unit with baits and roach spray and gave them a can to spray if needed. Just in case. I don't know why they didn't have a problem because the other unit literally had thousands of roaches running around.

Feeling beaten by the bugs, I went to the local store to pick up some supplies, figuring I might be able to salvage the day if I did some repair work despite the roaches. To my surprise, when I returned, Jackie was in the unit, showing it to a guy who owned a local Mexican restaurant. I watched the two of them walk around the unit, Jackie explaining how everything was going to go down. He saw roaches. I'm certain of that. He *had* to. They were *everywhere*.

Still, he paid Jackie a $300 deposit to hold the unit for two weeks, explaining that he planned on putting employees in the unit. The two of them shook hands and he left.

"You must've overwhelmed him with your charm," I told my wife. I just couldn't believe this guy would actually want a place that maybe could have been condemned.

If you don't know what an infestation looks like, imagine a horror film. Imagine opening every door and having roaches falling into your hair. Think of that scene in Indiana Jones and the Temple of Doom. You know the one. Yeah. An infestation is like that. The very floor writhes and crawls.

So I couldn't believe that my wife could rent that place out. What a saleswoman!

Unfortunately, the guy never showed up to take possession of the unit within the two weeks. This was a good and a bad, I guess: a good in that it gave me time to fix up the unit and get the roach situation under control; a bad in that we now had to find another tenant. That and Jackie could no longer gloat about how she sold a guy on an infested place.

In any case, true to form, in two weeks, I had the place looking much better. After all the work I had put into our properties, I was now pretty good at rehabilitation, after all. And I felt like Lord of the Cockroaches.

The (Failed) Construction Company

My confidence was growing. I figured that I could parlay all my recent rehabilitation success into a little sideline construction business. Actually, it's not appropriate to say it like that. Rather, I decided that our flipping houses and apartments revenue would increase dramatically if I could get a good construction and renovation team working for me.

So I began by hiring a few local guys to handle some day labor for me. As it turned out, they were all Mexican.

My first hire was a guy named Juan, a charming young guy Jackie and I had known from a nearby restaurant called La Palacia. He had long hair that he always tied in the back. The way I came to hiring him is that, one day, he came by and asked if I had any work because he had gotten fired for being late. I agreed and showed him how to install vinyl siding. I then dusted off my hands, happy to have gotten out of such tedious labor for the day.

I left for a while, and by the time I came back, Juan had finished the job. I was so impressed that I kept inviting him back to help me almost every day. But like many day laborers, he worked for about three months and then disappeared. I would come to find out later that he had a problem with drinking and driving and had gotten into trouble yet again.

I guess word had gotten around at La Palacia, because about two weeks later the manager there called and said that his cousin, Sergio, needed a job. I learned that he had worked as a laborer for an electrician and knew how to pull wire. My ears perked up at that. So I got Sergio started on vinyl siding and then trained him on everything from plumbing to electrical.

Sergio soon finished the vinyl siding job, so I put him to work on demolishing the floor of a termite-infested house I had recently purchased for a mere $15,000. He was a hard worker, but I know this work would be overwhelming. The next day, he came to work with a friend of his (another Mexican), a guy who liked to wear a Texas cowboy hat. His name also happened to be Juan. Yeah, it was confusing to me, too, but there was one key way to tell the two Juans apart: Unlike the first Juan, this Juan cussed a lot. Plus, he didn't seem to like to put in any actual work. Whenever I came back to check progress on the house, he always seemed to be on break.

The following Monday, the new Juan brought along his brother Charlie, who had a lot of construction experience. I explained to the three of them that I wanted to remove all of the rotten wood, but didn't really know how to accomplish it. Well, they made great progress and even

191

solved a problem that I didn't know how to solve on my own. By the time I returned to the site that afternoon, they had used my car jacks to install 4x4 beams to support the roof. I was happy and proud of my little construction team.

By the end of the week, they had removed all the flooring and interior walls. The only thing left was the shell of the home and the ceiling that was supported by 4x4 posts. You could jump down through what used to be the floor and walk around the inside on the dirt-lined crawl space.

My next step was to show them how to lay the floor joist on a central beam. They copied my instruction perfectly – and within two weeks, the floor joist was installed on the footings. As soon as they finished the floor joist installation, they began to put in the 31/4 inch plywood floor decking. It was pretty amazing, their progress.

But not all was harmonious. By the time we had reached this part of the job, I had noticed a little tension. As I mentioned, Juan was a little lazier than the other two workers. Eventually, it seemed as if he had been relegated to working outside (loading the dumpster) while Sergio and Charlie worked inside.

Repair and Renovations Lesson #7: If you plan on hiring out some of your labor, don't plan on everything going entirely smoothly. Sometimes, people just get tired of each other. Sometimes, fights and disputes will be commonplace.

The whole process took about a month. For less than $5,000, these three men had rebuilt most of the house. The entire rehab, materials included, cost only $10,000. The great thing was that I had long since paid off the $15,000 mortgage on the house and had managed to pay for labor and materials as I went, using income from other rental properties.

Apart from the new flooring and walls, we also installed new everything in the bathroom and kitchen. We also remodeled the kitchen slightly, as it used to have a door that opened to a dining room (even though the house also had a dining niche). We walled off this door and made what used to be the dining room into an extra bedroom.   Jackie and I were truly amazed at how beautiful this three-bedroom house turned out.

At this point, I realized that if I could keep a construction company working on our rehab houses, then whenever I needed to turn an apartment over, I could pull them off construction for a couple of days and put them on apartment cleaning/renovating detail. Plus, I knew that if I made an extra effort to teach our laborers construction and renovation details, they would be able to finish just about any project without my having to be there all the time. So I taught them about wiring and plumbing, all the finer details they hadn't been taught before.

This whole training process took about a month (and I had my guys working on a number of houses we had recently purchased). By the time we had renovated our next house, I began talking to Jackie about expanding our house-flipping operations. She didn't think it was a good idea, but I was seeing dollar signs.

So I got Sergio and took him down to a lot that held two houses for sale. The cost for both places together was

$42,000. I figured I could renovate and sell them for $190,000, but I needed to know if Sergio and his friends would be willing to help. Sergio agreed. He and the others promised to stay on for two months to help finish these jobs.

I was *really* seeing stars. I honestly started pricing a limo. If I could keep the construction company running, I realized, I could afford the limo. And I could even pay my construction workers as drivers.

So with our new lot and our two new houses, I decided to work on the bigger house first. As soon as Sergio, Charlie, Juan, and I started work, a guy named Phillip showed up, asking for a job. He was tall, smart, hard-working, and looked like an actor. He didn't speak English, so Sergio had to translate for him. But his presence was welcome because it freed up Sergio to work solely on the electrical.

We ended up taking the walls down to the studs, so it was a good opportunity to replace the windows and wiring. The large house had a very old slate roof, which might have been nice except that all the pieces were brittle and broken. So we had to clear it off.

One day, I was on the property while the guys were clearing debris from around the building. They were watching me cut tree limbs with a chainsaw when I fell through the roof, up to my chest. My arms and head were the only things supporting me from falling the rest of the way down. The chainsaw kept buzzing near my head as I struggled to free myself. I remember being terrified at first and then laughing like a maniac.

Below, I could see the workers running around, bumping into each other in a panic. Pretty comical.

It was a miracle I wasn't hurt. They pulled me out of the roof and I immediately told them to rip the damn thing down. From then on, I could tell that they didn't want me on the roof. I guess they were worried about losing their employer (to say nothing of their steady payday).

Soon thereafter, Sergio asked for a $500 advance so he could buy a red truck from Lazy Juan's son, Israel. I had known Israel for years – a handsome guy who waited tables at La Palacia. I figured since I knew both parties, it couldn't hurt to give my best worker the advance he needed.

Sergio was so proud when he drove up in his new red truck. He used it on site for several days that week. But we would come to find out later that the business transaction didn't go over so well with Lazy Juan, who was angry with his son for selling the truck for so cheap. Apparently, he had beaten up Sergio in retribution. Jackie and I were stunned.

The next day, I went to the apartment that I was renting to my workers and only Lazy Juan was left. Charlie, Phillip, and Sergio had left in the middle of the night.

"Gone to Washington State," Juan said.

They had driven off in the red truck that Sergio had just purchased. Purchased with my advance payment. *Damn!*

Jackie and the boys were with me when I told Juan he couldn't live in Sergio's apartment – that he had to leave and go live with his son, Israel. With all of us working together, it was a pretty easy move-out. I gave Juan a couple of trash bags for his clothes, we hauled the furniture out to the dumpster, and in less than an hour, I had the locks changed.

Exasperated, I told Juan that I didn't have any more work for him. He looked crestfallen when I told him. I'm betting that he figured if he got rid of Sergio and the others, he and his family would assume control of the construction operation (as well as the apartment I'd just kicked him out of).

I can't tell you how sad Sergio's leaving made me. I felt betrayed. I couldn't imagine such an honorable worker doing this. It made my heart ache because I really loved the kid and even had thoughts of making him a partner in our house-flipping operation.

Later that night, we received word that Charlie would agree to come back if I bought him a truck, too. "No thanks," was our replay. Even though carrying the unfinished property without renting it would be a burden on us financially, we could afford it. The truly difficult part was to think that in one evening, my construction company, my limo, my team of drivers, and my piles of cash were all gone. These dreams had all driven up to Washington State with a truck full of Mexicans.

Pest Control

Let me just get one last thing off my chest before I close up this flipping houses chapter: Even if you do everything right, even if you get your construction down perfectly, you can still get screwed by one of the bundle of inspectors who has to examine the house before closing. That first house that I worked on with Sergio and company was a prime example...

So proud of our tireless and thorough work, Jackie and I listed the house with a great friend of ours who sells real estate. During the closing, we had to have a termite inspection. Now it is very important to recall that we had replaced every board in the flooring and foundation with pressure treated wood. I had poured poison into the foundation area during the construction, as well. But most importantly, while we were in the process of demolishing the building, we didn't find *any* termite activity. The soil and wood had a strong chemical smell and obviously had been treated very effectively in the past.

But Pest Control Lesson #1: Pest control guys might treat for rats, but they also *are* rats. Rats.

So it came as kind of a shock when Jackie called and said that the pest control guy had found termites.

"Tell him I'm on my way," I said.

Shortly after I put in the word that I was coming to check the inspector's work, the bastard changed his tune.

"Actually, I was mistaken," he said. "I didn't find termites."

"Well did you crawl under the house to check?" I asked.

No, he hadn't. Strange...

"Well I'll be over in a minute," I said. "If you find termites under that house, I'll crawl under there with you to see for myself."

He agreed to wait for me. When I arrived, I watched him crawl his fat ass under the house. By the time he had finished his inspection, he was a changed man. He'd found no termites to report. I could tell he was pissed, though. Must have been the first time he'd ever had a homeowner grab a light and follow him under a house.

Let me give you a little background on pest control motives. The termite guy charges $1,500 to treat a home. To treat a place, they use about $30 of poison concentrate and a few gallons of water from your spigot. Sometimes, they drill holes into hollow bricks and insert a chemical (which they use an impact drill and minimum wage help to do). So in the end, a termite control company can clear over $1,200 on most homes...but only if they actually *find* termites. So the motivation to "find" them is pretty heavy.

Later on, after I had completed another flip house, we had the same company inspect for termites. Much to my chagrin, they sent over the same guy. I wasn't surprised in the least when he came around from behind the house, all smiles.

"Termites," he said.

"You're kidding," I said. I just couldn't believe it. I mean, this house did have a crawl space beneath it at about seven feet tall. You could stand up underneath the house. Being sixty years old, it *did* have some termite damaged wood along the vent holes where some old wooden windows had been installed many years ago, but I hadn't replaced it because it was such insignificant wood.

Termite Guy took me up to one of the boards in the crawl space. "Look right there," he said.

I looked and saw a single larvae with its tail squished onto the surface of the brick. On the ground, he managed to show me one more sitting right on top of the dirt. Two termite larvae in the entire crawl space.

"How much will it cost to treat down here?" I asked.

"Oh, we can't treat down here," he said.

I looked around. It was an enormous crawl space. The idea that they couldn't get their equipment in there was ridiculous. "My God, you could drive a truck under here. It'd be easy."

I started digging in the area where the two larvae were found. I excavated a three foot circle on the inside and the outside of the wall and didn't find any more. I mean, if this was a viable colony, then these two larvae should have had a host of mature adults tending to them. But I found nothing. Not one termite.

Naturally, I was pissed. Termite Guy knew he had me because his inspection was the only thing we were waiting for before we could close on the house.

I knew that if I called another pest control company, Termite Guy would circumvent me and check with the new owner to see if the house had been treated. "No?" he would say. "But I found termites." I could just see it: Termite Guy trying to make it look like I had been unscrupulous.

So I knew I'd been set up. He wasn't going to let me make a liar out of him. I even began to suspect that the larvae had been planted. After all, I didn't find any evidence of additional bugs – and you know what? He tore ass out of there as soon as I began digging. I never saw him at that house again.

I got a call from Juan soon after saying that Termite Guy wanted to get under the adjacent house, which we also owned. I was a block away when I got the call, so I hopped in the truck and pulled up to the adjacent house.

"What are you doing?" I asked.

"I just wanted to take a look at this other house," he said, looking incredibly guilty. "You're going to sell it, too, right?"

I didn't reply.

"I can go ahead and look at it now," he offered.

"You can look now," I said, "but I'm coming in with you."

Nervously, he checked his watch. "Oops," he said lamely. "I don't have time right now."

I guess he just didn't want to do the inspection with me watching.

I had Juan replace the wood in the crawl space vents, so he was the one who had to do all the extra work. From then on, I made it a point to do a personal inspection and pour powerful, stinky-ass poison into the area of the crawl space before any inspection. I also drilled the block and put poison in the foundation prior to the arrival of any Termite Guys. I also made sure that I or one of my employees was always with the inspector during their inspections.

I never had another problem with the crooked termite guys. So there's your final lesson, reader: When flipping houses and apartments, it's important to keep a sharp eye.

Not just a sharp eye for termites, but a sharp eye from every angle of your property, your building, your business. Maybe you've seen the cable television shows that make flipping houses look easy. First you find a house you think can sell; you purchase it, fix it up, and sell it the day you finish, right? As you've seen, it just isn't that easy, and you'll almost never be that lucky. But remember: luck can bring success and success can bring opportunity – and perhaps more importantly, lots of cool shit!

Chapter Seven

Movin' On Up

I know this will probably sound kind of pathetic considering all this tough-guy rental stuff, but my little tomboy wife had gotten all prissy on me. She was getting pedicures, manicures, massages, and pining for a convertible. I guess I can't blame her. By the time we were ready to start thinking about movin' on up to a more polished rental game, we had more money than we ever thought possible.

I was so happy the day I bought Jackie her silver convertible. Even she was shocked by the degree that she loved it. Tears streamed down her face when we drove it home from the dealership with the top down.

Not coincidentally, the week we bought the convertible, we also realized that we finally had enough financial clout at the banks to try for a first class property. Like I said: movin' on up. We had dreams of a smooth transaction with an honest businessman. We fantasized about what it would be like to collect rent from people with jobs, rather than people on welfare and disability. We envisioned a bright future of rent checks and hassle-free tenants.

Boy, were we wrong.

Jackie had her eye on an apartment complex owned by Thomas Means. I've got to give my wife credit, she was aiming high: this complex was easily the nicest in the area. *And* she had an in. See, she had gotten to know Means because he owned a trailer business. A while previous, Jackie had helped her mother to secure a trailer for Melinda, a woman who had worked for Jackie's family for over thirty years. Jackie was only three when Melinda first took the job for her mother, so she was very dear to my wife and close to her heart. Helping her to buy a trailer seemed like the least we could do.

See, Melinda's husband had recently died. And during her marriage, she had gone through some tough and hard times, anyway. Melinda confided to Jackie that she felt she couldn't go back to the house she had shared with her husband because of all the bad memories. Not to mention that the house was a wooden shack with dirt floors. And also not to mention that Melinda was terribly superstitious.

Having found his ad in the newspaper and given him a quick appraising call, Jackie recommended Thomas Means' trailer business to her mother. She even went down to the lot with her mom and Melinda, introducing them both to Means. They looked at several trailers before Melinda completely fell in love with a beautiful new 4-bedroom, 2-bath home. It seemed perfect for her family.

Jackie's mom purchased the trailer home so Melinda could live there. Means then made arrangements for the trailer to be delivered to Melinda's lot in Jackson Town, Alabama. Melinda ecstatically moved in, seeming unable to believe her good fortune.

About two months later – on a day when it was more than a hundred degrees outside – Melinda called Jackie, upset because Means refused to return her calls about the trailer's air conditioner having crapped out. Word had it from Melinda that Means had been rude about the whole thing.

Jackie couldn't stand the thought of Melinda suffering in the heat, so she decided to do something about it. Plus, this was supposed to be a brand new trailer. Problems with air conditioners shouldn't have been an issue. So Jackie took off to talk to Thomas. She drove to his business and demanded to speak to him right away. Heading into his office, she told him the only reason she had brought her mother into his business to buy a mobile home was because she thought Means would stand behind his product. She told him that he best get someone out there and get the unit fixed immediately.

"It's probably just the air filter," Means said with a dismissive wave. "It's her responsibility to change it."

Jackie calmly informed Means that Melinda had never had the comfort of central heat and air in her life and that she wouldn't know about air filters. My wife expected this shady dealer to get off his ass and get it fixed. "I wouldn't have recommended you if I'd known what kind of businessman you are," she said. Then, she stormed out.

Jackie got the call from Melinda at about 5pm that same day.

"I don't know what you said to Thomas," Melinda said, "but he came out and fixed the air himself."

Jackie kept a standing line open to Melinda, telling her former caregiver that if she had any more problems, she knew who to call. That's my wife. The enforcer.

She also knows compassion and gratefulness, does Jackie. She called Means and told him that she appreciated his promptness in taking care of the air conditioner situation. It was important to know that Means could be counted on to right a wrong. But then, we probably should have paid better attention to the fact that he'd sold a trailer with a bum air conditioner. That he'd sold us something that wasn't quite what it seemed...

You know where this is going. The time came when we were in the market for a nice apartment complex. Lo and behold, Thomas Means was in the complex business. Jackie called to find out if one of his properties was for sale. He informed that everything he owned was for sale. She made an appointment with him, and in short order, we managed to buy a 20-unit complex with a swimming pool and a laundry room.

So here's **Movin' on Up Lesson #1**: If you do a smaller deal with a dishonest businessman, why would you turn around and do a larger one?

Yep, we were movin' on up.

Carriage Hills – The "Dream" Complex

Ah, Carriage Hills. Things started out auspiciously enough. Our spankin' new apartment complex was in a great location on Highway 110 – within walking distance of the school, a golf course, and of course, the K-Mart Supercenter. When we inherited the place, the units were full of professional people – nurses, engineers, teachers, and store managers.

We were delighted because every month the tenants put their rent checks in the drop box by the 5th of the month. Each month, twenty checks, around $400 each, could be found in the drop box. So, we picked up around $8,000 dollars a month from this complex, right out of the box. If a tenant was late, they would pay the late fees, no questions asked.

It was great to acquire this property at that time in our lives. We were clearing $2,000 right at closing and we got almost $5,000 for deposit escrow. Thomas Means even kept an office at the complex and continued to stay for a couple of years, helping us to smooth over the transition.

Well, let me tell you we had some real winners. Seriously. Many of these tenants rented from us for over ten years – great people; no trouble at all. To this day, we talk about some of them and hope they are all well and happy.

But despite the prompt rent payments, despite the glowing and respectful attitudes, despite the seemingly charmed existence of Carriage Hills, they weren't all quite what they seemed...

The Pederast

We had one tenant, a teacher, who rented from us for almost fifteen years. In addition to teaching at the nearby high school, he was a coach for the girls' softball team. Everyone liked the guy. He seemed like the perfect tenant, never complaining, always on the road with his team. It wasn't unusual for me to be in Birmingham or Hattisburg when someone would overhear my conversation about being from Hasselville and ask me if I knew this coach. I would always say that I did; and they would always proceed to tell me what a great guy he was.

So imagine how startled Jackie and I were when we received his 30-day notice to leave. Startled isn't really the right word. Not at first, anyway. We were surprised at first, assuming that Coach had finally decided to buy a home instead of continuing to rent for us. The startled part came when we found out the reason for Coach's leaving was not the purchase of a new home.

He moved out quickly, leaving nothing (not even a mess) behind.

Turns out old Coach liked to call the young girls on his team all the time. *All* the time. Something happened with one of them, I've heard, because he had to resign his job and leave Hasselville. One day at work, Jackie was talking to a coworker who knew him. This coworker had daughters in the school, she couldn't stand Coach, and thought he was weird.

Pederast Lesson #1: Never trust a pervert. Not even with the rent.

Looking back, I never saw this strange tenant out with a grown woman. He was a bachelor and spent all his time on the road with schoolgirls. Just so typical. You have to wonder how long all those calls went on to the young girls before someone stood up and put a stop to it.

The Cat Man

Two doors down from the Coach, we had a renter named Mr. Bender. He was the only one in the whole complex consistently late on the rent. Jackie would have to call him at work every month. He was always very apologetic about being late and always had his excuses (he had problems with his car, his bonus checks, his car, his bonus checks, etc.). Every time, he would get caught up by the 20th of the following month.

The guy was a youth minister and wrote a newsletter type bulletin for the church. He would write all these inspiring messages and words of wisdom with his picture right beside his name. He was over 6 feet tall, bald and had a slight hump when he walked. Jackie always called him "Lurch" because he reminded her of the character from The Adams Family with the exception that Lurch had a hell of a lot more personality. "Lurch" really creeped her out. In addition to all that, he seemed like a nice guy because he loved animals, especially cats. He was a single guy, and when he moved in, he brought with him two of the most beautiful long-haired cats I had ever seen.

One day, I was making my rounds to change air filters. I opened his door and noticed that his apartment was filled with clutter and that he had put a mattress on the floor downstairs in the living room. As I walked in, I noticed that he had turned the entire floor in the galley kitchen into a litter/food box. The *entire* floor. It was pretty disgusting. I left a note for him to get his place cleaned up. When he didn't respond, Jackie called him at work to tell him about it.

"I know," he said. "Just settling in. Working long hours. I'll take care of it."

In the months to come, Mr. Bender never called with maintenance problems and so we never had any need to enter the apartment until it was time to do our regular maintenance work. I went back to the apartment a couple months later to change the air filter again. Surprise, surprise, I found that the unit was in horrible condition. I don't know if Bender was mad at us or just crazy, but he seemed to have quit changing the litter box completely. I couldn't get into the kitchen because the trash and litter was knee deep. In every corner, there was cat shit. In the dining room and in the living room, piss was sprayed all over the walls. One corner of his mattress was coated with shit and piss.

217

The Cat Man Lesson #1: These lonely cat-people can be a problem.   Particularly if they have more than two cats. Cats do damage like no other.

I did a head count. Both his cats had had kittens, so now there were two cats and fifteen kittens. On one wall, I found a brown smear in the shape of a hand print. It looked as if Bender had put his hand down in shit when getting up and instead of washing it in the sink; he had wiped it on the wall. Seriously, reader. Seriously.

I don't know how he could live with these cats, much less sleep with them. It was gross, creepy, and to tell the truth, a little frightening.

Eventually, he got to where he would just leave the back sliding glass door to his apartment open so his cats could roam the complex. At night, he would take a chair out to the edge of the woods and sit with all the cats moving on him and around him. Freaking *weird!*

He called us one night, horrified and in tears because a rattlesnake had killed one of his cats. Another time, a cat got into the hot water compartment of the laundry room, and instead of calling me, he kicked the door in to free the little bastard. Later, he sent me a letter saying that I should keep the door closed on the supply room door because a cat could get killed.

Of course we read him the riot act and he promised to give the kittens away and clean up the apartment.

I suppose you're wondering why we didn't just evict this loser. There are three reasons: first, he was part of the society of Hasselville; second, he was a respected writer; and third, the unit was ruined. Besides, the neighbors couldn't smell anything from the hallways or through their walls and never complained. I just tried to get the most out of his occupancy because I knew it was going to have to be gutted when he left. He agreed that when he left, he would pay for all the damages to the apartment.

Naturally, he didn't keep up his end of that bargain, so we had to take him to court. Jackie and I made a video of the mess he'd left, but we were not allowed to show it in court. On the day of the hearing, Jackie decided to take our boys along so they could witness a grown man not taking responsibility for his actions. The boys had assisted us in cleaning up the mess, see. They were around thirteen years old at the time – and ready for justice, as we considered the place their property, as well.

Mr. Bender had hired an attorney and we would find out that he'd filed for bankruptcy. Of course, the judge didn't award us anything. It was over as quickly as Jackie and the boys sat down in the courtroom. Jackie tried to make eye contact with Mr. Bender, but he never looked back.

So we went to court and found that no justice was served there. But I'll get my satisfaction by describing more of Mr. Bender's living conditions to you. Here's a rundown of the day I went into the unit to document the damage.

Eight full grown cats were running around everywhere. He had moved his shitty/pissy mattress upstairs, apparently to get away from the disturbing mess that was now all over the walls, especially in the corners. The carpets were completely covered in trampled-over, decomposing cat shit and urine. Even though I was holding my nose and breathing through my mouth, it was amazing that I could manage to do my inventory without passing out.

Naturally, the first step in renovating this cat-hole was to rip up the carpet throughout the apartment. In case you don't know this already, carpeting has a foam pad that runs underneath it. It's used for cushion, but it's just like a sponge. So it had to go. Imagine what it looked like, months and months of cat piss...

My boys and I wore gloves and dust masks as we worked. We cut the pad and the carpet into two-foot-long rolls and bagged all the material for the dumpster. Even though we cleaned the walls and floor with bleach, we could still smell the urine. Frustrated but not deterred, I ordered some kind of cleaning enzyme from a floor care company. This stuff is typically used to clean up biological material and is designed to remove the proteins that create odor. The enzyme helped, and after it dried, we put plastic down and installed laminate flooring. We then painted the walls with an epoxy paint called Kilz.

The apartment was beautiful by the time we'd finished, but we still caught the occasional whiff of cat urine when we walked through.

Angry now, I came up with the idea of burning scented candles in the corners and closets where the cats had marked their territory (and possibly where Mr. Bender himself had marked his). We ran the candles. Then, Jackie re-applied bleach to the corners of each wall and we repainted after it dried. Finally, the smell was gone and we were left with a great apartment. It was a lot of work, but in the end, we were able to raise the rent over $100 a month.

I heard later that after Bender filed bankruptcy, the slob quit his job and took one with the competing paper. I imagine he had several garnishments coming out of his paycheck. Turns out he beat a lot of people out of money. No one said anything. They read his stories, sat at his table for lunch, and worst of all, shook his hand (Gross!). Everyone got screwed, but he still stumbles around town to this day. When I see him in a restaurant, he will always leave. What a nut-job.

The Interior Decorator

The tenant before the blind lady was a college student from a very nice family. She moved into the apartment and painted all the walls. She tried every technique and the brightest colors. In one room she painted the wall and trim fire engine red. Another room was painted 3 shades of green. Paint was all over the carpet and it was one big mess.

The Interior Decorator Lesson #1: No matter how black and white you make it in the contract, some tenants just won't be happy with black and white décor. You can tell them not to paint. That doesn't mean they won't paint. Keep some spare, heavy-duty white paint at hand. You'll need it.

The term of our standard lease is for one year. After the year, the tenancy goes from month to month, with a 30 day written notice requirement of intention to vacate. The lease term ends on the last day of the month and new tenants begin their lease on the first day of the month. Often, tenants would try to stay a couple of days into the next month, causing problems with turnover. We required the notice of intention to vacate so we could show the apartment and lease it to a new tenant who had to move in on the first of the month.

One of the best ways to defeat a lease is for tenants to claim they had been burglarized. If safety is a problem, the court and judges will not make them fulfill the contract. Usually, someone like us would not want any publicity, because this might cause mass panic at a complex. People could just bolt or simply claim that danger is the reason they shouldn't have to fulfill the lease.

This interior designer wannabe called Jackie and told her someone had broken into her apartment. She had previously turned in a notice but was responsible for the rent after the notice. Jackie told her to call the police, report it and that I would be over to fix the door. She said she didn't want to call the police because nothing was missing and there is no damage. By the way, reporting a fabricated break in to the police is a felony.

I called her back and talked with her. I asked how she knew her apartment had been broken into? She said she found doo-doo in her toilet and it hadn't been flushed. I asked her if it could have been her fiancé, who I knew to be at her unit sometimes if she were out of town. She also said one of the flowers she had hot glued to the shower curtain had fallen off and that is how she knew she had been burglarized. She said maybe it was someone who worked for me and asked me if any workers had keys to her apartment.

At that time, Jackie and I handled all the apartment maintenance by our selves and no one else had keys to any of the apartments. And if I did need extra help, I would be with the person who helped me. She later called Jackie and told her she no longer felt safe in the unit and was moving out without the responsibility of notice. Neither Jackie nor I wanted her running around town saying it wasn't safe to live in our apartments because our employees were taking dumps and possibly showers in the apartments. We let her walk right over us. We played it cool but it really pissed us off.

Yep, she moved right into the house she had been trying to close on for 3 months. One again we celebrated losing a nut tenant. It didn't cost her a thing. Jackie returned her deposit in full. We lost a month's rent, plus the cost for repainting her mess on the walls and replacing the carpet. Jackie showed her the hallway where paint went half way up and asked her if she was going to fix it before she left. She replied with her fake beauty queen smile "Oh no, I can't reach it". You think you know someone and then for a few hundred dollars or less they pull a stunt like that. Her family had money and social status in the community and there is no excuse for her to handle business the way she did. Spreading a rumor like this could have had devastating effects on our tiny business.

Fraud

Call this closing story icing on the cake. Just when we were starting to kind of get the hang of dealing with the new breed of weirdoes and losers you get when you own an apartment complex, a nice little shitstorm rolled in on us.

I remember the day I received a letter from a company called Monseco. The letter? Monesco had placed a lien on our new twenty-unit apartment complex. Needless to say, I was shocked. And a little woozy.

Obviously, my first step in a situation like this one was to head straight for the lawyer's office, so I paid a visit to the attorney who had closed our deal at the time of purchase. Here's another one for the pool of anti-attorney sentiment: Our lawyer had lost the deed. His offices had filed the mortgage but not the deed on the apartments. Of course, no one told us this. Until Monesco came calling, that is...

I was speechless. In the eyes of my bank, I owed $500,000 on Carriage Hills Apartments; but in the eyes of the law, I didn't own the property.

As I mentioned earlier, we bought Carriage Hills from Thomas Means, a man who was also in the trailer business. Apparently, he had done great during the boom. Later, I was told by a self titled "private detective" that the sales reps at the trailer dealerships had been printing phony documents for buyers off the internet. The loans these phony documents produced were made by an insurance group called Monesco. The whole scheme *really* fueled trailer sales in the area. I don't have any reason to believe that this is true other than what the investigator told me "off the record". It was the "sub-prime trailer" disaster!

So I guess greedy Thomas stayed in the business too long. His buyers began to default on their loans – loans they never would have qualified for but for the fraud.

From what I understand, this kind of thing isn't unusual. In fact, it runs in cycles. From what I'm told, if you know when to get out of the business, you can turn a nice profit on a scam like this. All you have to do is lay low for a while. Then, after a couple of years, you can get back in. During the off times, the shady trailer dealer can continue to rake in scratch by buying into commercial property. Carriage Hills Apartments was apparently Thomas' off-cycle business venture.

Rumor had it that Thomas was also ordering trailers and then not paying for them. He would string his creditors out for months. I guess that at the time he sold us the apartments, he was desperate for cash. Obviously, Thomas disappeared not long after the sale. Meanwhile, we were left cleaning up his messes. See, Monseco placed a lien on all his property in Escambia and surrounding counties. Because of the screw-up by our lawyer, "all his property" included Carriage Hills, a place we'd thought we'd owned for two years already.

This was all around the same time the slob cat man had beaten us out of our damages through the glory of bankruptcy, so we were in no position to take on a huge monetary hit. We had worked so hard and it looked like we were just about to lose our first legitimately decent property.

Clearly, I was devastated. It felt like we were never going to get ahead. It just seemed so surreal to think that a clerical error could cost us the property.

The attorney was just as upset. "Pat," she said, "I assure you that I have enough insurance to cover your losses."

Noble of her. I mean, I had only paid her $500 to close the place for us and here she was willing to risk it all to right the wrong. Maybe attorneys aren't so bad. She had her reasons, I'm sure. I mean, I think we were some of her first clients, as she was new in town.

Anyway, it wouldn't come to that. She would work with another attorney; this one named Woodman (both of them were smart as a whip, incidentally) and they would work it out in the Circuit Court. In the end, we wound up maintaining ownership of Carriage Hills Apartments. But man, what a headache.

Woodman had taken care of the problem in about sixty days. He wouldn't take any money, either. He was our hero. Now that we've done so much business with him (and he has impressed us thoroughly every time), looking back, I realize that Woodman was probably the only person around who could have pulled this off. I learned my lesson and have used him for all my closings ever since.

Once the judge issued his ruling, we had the best kind of deed. It settled every issue in one final stroke. I have to admit that I had begun to get a pretty low opinion of attorneys, judges, and the court system in general. I thank Woodman for changing my opinion and keeping me optimistic about the court system.

I am not sure what happened to Thomas. Rumor has it that he served some jail time, but I doubt it. We learned all this information and then some from Rusty Davis the man who took care of our lawns at Carriage Hill and who had taken care of the lawns under Thomas' regime, as well. Some time later, Davis told us that Thomas had opened a trailer lot in Leedstown. He'd hired a dealer who sold a trailer on the first day on the job. When Thomas refused to pay him until he sold his second trailer, the dealer got pissed. *Really* pissed. Evidently, the dealer beat the shit out of Thomas. He broke his ribs, blackened his eye, and broke his collarbone.

When I was first dealing with Thomas, I thought he was on his way to being the South's Donald Trump. I guess I should have known better. If you're willing to screw your elderly yard man out of his pay, you can't get far. That's just Karma, as Jackie would say.

231

As I said before, success can bring you lots of opportunity. Jackie and I had the opportunity to buy more and, as a result, receive bigger returns on our investments. Seems reasonable. But with more money comes more responsibility and more problems. Just like in any business, the more you own, the more you have to manage, and that takes some getting used to.

Chapter Eight

Emergency Maintenance Calls

Here's the deal with owning large apartment complexes: more tenants might mean more money, but it also means more "emergency" maintenance calls. I put emergency in quotes because sometimes emergencies aren't exactly emergencies, if you catch my drift. Sometimes, you'll wind up picking up the phone at 3am just to go down to one of your buildings and unclog a toilet. Some people are crazy. Some are helpless. You just have to roll with the punches.

But let me tell you, you get to know the patterns. There are days when the calls start ringing more often. Days when you might as well just wait by the phone. Weekends are usually busier in the maintenance department, which I guess makes sense, given that everyone in the family is home all day, examining everything, pining for that little flaw they can call to complain about. Gives them something to do, I guess. Holidays, though, are the worst. You'll probably be able to enjoy your Christmas. Maybe your Thanksgiving. But on all the national holidays, forget it.

Memorial Day, Labor Day, any three-day weekend, really. Still, as bad as those three-day-ers may get to be, none is worse than the one that happens in early July...

Independence Day

When you're in the landlording business, the name for this national holiday gets to be kind of ironic. It's a day to celebrate our nation's independence from tyranny, but seeing as how all your tenants are going to be having friends over...grilling out...drinking...drinking...drinking...you're not exactly going to feel like you've got your *own* independence. Your tenants are going to seem pretty damned dependent on you, anyway.

Anyway, let's get down to our little parables regarding this day of days. We had a unit open in one of our duplexes and we leased it to a lady named Pam, who was from the neighboring Sumter County. Pam had a common-law husband named Robert, and even though there were two of them, they had a little trouble with rent in the first few months. I guess Pam had to get all her welfare information transferred to Escambia County (No, when you move up to owning higher-end apartments, you aren't immune to welfare tenants). My wife the enforcer was integral in getting all that bad noise sorted out for Pam and Robert. She drove them all over both counties so they could make whatever transactions go along with transferring welfare benefits.

I don't mean to give a wrong impression, though. We liked Pam and Robert very much. They rented from us for years. But they did have one major flaw: come the 4th of July, they would turn into raving lunatics.

I think Pam must have had us on speed dial. Every Fourth, she'd call up and complain about something. She would inevitably be pissed off and want to know whether Robert was on the lease with her (every Fourth, she'd wind up wanting to kick the poor bastard out of the apartment). Of course, this would always upset Jackie and I – they were such a nice couple, after all – and we would try to figure out what to do, but by Monday (always by Monday), they would be back to loving each other again.

It took us a couple of years to realize that this little spat was just part of their celebration. We came to realize that that sort of thing was part of everyone's celebration.

Emergency Maintenance Calls Lesson #1: The Fourth of July brings out the worst in people. They get together in large groups (often with people they haven't seen since the last Independence Day), drink their faces off, and start getting rowdy. This leads to either actual damage or drunken-imaginary damage. Either way, expect your phone to ring.

Once we'd learned Lesson #1, we could relax when the phone would ring – particularly when the caller ID showed that it was Pam. I remember the first year after our realization very vividly.

"Hello Pam," I said when I answered the phone, the sultry smell of grilled steaks wafting in from outside.

"Patrick," she barked, all in a huff, "Who's on our lease again? I just wanna get Robert outta here."

"Okay, Pam," I said calmly. "I tell you what: I'll come over on Monday after lunch and see how you feel. If you still want him out, I'll work it out with both of you."

Pam laughed her cackling laugh. "You right, Patrick. Okay, thank you."

I guess she finally figured out she did this every Independence Day.

You have to realize the degree of 4th of July celebrations in areas of low income tenants. It gets bad in the upper end places, too, but areas like our Walnut Street properties get out of control. Celebration is heavy. Great big barbeque pits are fired up between units, card tables arranged, kids running everywhere and playing with hoses and sprinklers. For the most part, it's a wonderful time. But sometimes, all hell breaks loose. Tempers flare. Fights break out. The shit really hits the fan.

But as I said, come Monday morning, everyone's usually happy and friendly again.

As for Pam and Robert, they would have conversations for years to come about their 4th of July celebrations. Jackie always liked going over there to get the rent around that time because Robert could cook and they were always offering food. Jackie liked to have a beer and talk to Pam and Christy. Our boys liked to run around in the sprinklers with all the other children, too.

Dinnertime

I bet if you were to ask any person with rental property what is the most common time for an emergency maintenance call, they would agree that it's dinnertime. I'm not sure what it is about that particular hour, but it's magical. Problems just always seem to crop up the moment you sit down to eat.

I remember renting a unit to a young woman who worked at the hospital. She was a fine tenant until she got pregnant and had a baby. One night, it snowed three inches in Hasselville, which is very uncommon. We might get a snow that will stick about once every five years.

Well, this young lady took a roommate – a big girl – and around dinnertime, this big girl went to take a bath. Long story short: she twisted the hot water knob and stem right out of the wall. Water began shooting straight out and flooded down the wall to the ground floor. A neighbor tried to cut the water off, but found that the handle was missing. So the entire downstairs flooded.

I arrived a few minutes after the call came through. Shut the water off and repaired the stem. But I was there until 3am trying to get the water out of the building. The doors were open for airflow and I swept excess water right out the door. Remember, it was cold enough for snow, so it was downright freezing that night. But I was determined to save the carpet. The girl took her baby to her mother's house and stayed there. This was fine with me, as I was afraid I was going to have to pay for a hotel room for her. This would have been especially bad because I wasn't sure of my housing liability for her. I mean, she was a month behind on the rent – was I supposed to pay $80 per night for her to sleep in a hotel?

But no rest for the wicked. I got home around 3:30, made

some coffee, and got ready for work. Yep. It was winter, it was snowing, I was running on zero sleep, and it was deer season. I had to leave on patrol at 5 AM.

The girl stayed with her mother for a couple of days until the apartment dried enough for her to return. She never complained. I guess she was glad that we were willing to work with her on the rent.

That girl had the worst luck. She got back into her apartment and it wasn't two months before she was pregnant again. We never saw a guy at her apartment, so we never met the babies' daddies. Then, while she was at work one day, a couple she had brought in to help her cover the rent went through her personal things and found her social security card, birth certificate, and checkbook. They rented a bunch of furniture and got credit cards in her name. Basically, they completely destroyed her credit. Some time later, the couples' picture showed up in the paper. They had been identified as professional identity thieves.

The Chronic Complainer

During the nineties, we had an influx of immigrants from Pakistan, India, and Russia come into our small southern town. This was great because many of them turned out to be excellent businesspeople. Many local hotels are now owned by Indian or Pakistani families. Our Fendley's sandwich shop was purchased by a Pakistani family, as well.

Anyway, that's beside the point. We're talking about tenants here.

A couple from India (with new baby) moved into one of our units. One day Darji, the proud new father, called and wanted a larger refrigerator. I told him I would have to charge more rent to upgrade, so he decided that what they had was fine. It was brand new, but just fifteen cubic feet. I'm getting off on a bit of tangent, here, but this bit pissed me off about Darji, so I'm going to tell it anyway:

About two weeks later, my newest tenant called and told me that the refrigerator was broken. When I checked on it,

I found that they had pulled the gasket away from the door. I was pretty steamed. I told them that I would get them a new refrigerator, but that when their lease was up, they had to find another place to live.

They were not taken in kindly by their next door neighbor, either. A single woman, this neighbor. Let's call her Sally. Anyway, Sally started complaining about the noise and smells coming from Darji's apartment. At first, being that I was angry about the refrigerator incident, I figured that her complaints were sincere. Besides, Sally had been a good tenant for nearly seven years. So here's what I did: I bought her a tape recorder and told her to record the noises (supposedly the loudest noises Sally'd ever heard coming from an apartment).

Well, here's what happened: Sally kept complaining, the tape kept showing up empty...silent.

Still, we weren't about to disbelieve Sally. So Jackie called Darji and asked him to keep the noise down. He sounded confused, I'm told, but was nevertheless willing to be quiet, in future.

Sally continued to complain, even calling the police and our maintenance man. Nobody ever heard anything. Meanwhile, she never managed to record any sound.

I finally told Darji that his lease was up and the family needed to make other living arrangements. This seemed fine with Darji, as he was sick of getting the police called on him. Considering all the drama, he was happy to go.

Not long after being asked to leave, he informed us that he had found a house to move into. My wife met with him, cleared the apartment, and wrote him a check for the security deposit.

About two months later, Sally called and said she had to move out immediately because of stress. Jackie asked her where she was going.

"Oh," she said, "I'm closing on a house and moving into it on Saturday."

Ah-ha! All this nonsense now made perfect sense. Sally had been trying to close on the house for months and needed an excuse for immediate departure.

I felt bad about Darji and his family. He must have been totally confused.

I just couldn't help but dislike Sally for what she had done to us and to Darji. Well, guess what? Her house deal fell through. Again, Karma. Not long thereafter, she called us up, asking to return to her old unit. Jackie told her that the apartment was rented and that she had to get her things out.

"We let you out due to a stressful state of living, remember?" Jackie said. "It's too noisy and stressful for you to live here...remember?"

Once we knew the true score, we were sick about Darji and his family. We would find out later – after a chance encounter at the local Fendley's that the Darji family really loved their new home, though, so that made us feel better.

The Chronic Complainer Lesson #1: Not all tenant complaints are valid – especially the ones that come from people who complain all the time. Check them out thoroughly before acting on them. Maintain a policy of mild skepticism.

The takeaway message for this chapter, reader, is that you should never get too comfortable. Plan on disasters happening. Plan, also, to make visits to your rental units that you could have avoided if tenants, in general, weren't so needy (or otherwise ignorant about what does and does not make for an emergency maintenance call). Even the tenants you least expect to hassle you might wind up doing just that.

And as you'll see in the next chapter, that same lesson counts for your staff, as well.

Chapter Nine

Resident Managers

When you get involved with bigger complexes and you have to deal with more people, the work obviously gets a little out of hand. The natural response is to start hiring people to help you take care of all the bullshit. This is a good idea, but it still comes with a few cautionary tales. Bottom line: you have to be careful who you hire. You'll deal with the irresponsible. The snakes. The weirdoes. The general shitless layabouts.

The other point to consider when getting into larger complexes is that they often come complete with other services that you might not yet be used to. Pools, laundry rooms, fitness centers; they can all wind up being more work than they might be worth. Public space can be a money drain. It's most certainly a time drain. And you're going to wind up feeling as much like a cop as you are a landlord. Much of it proved too much for us to handle, anyway. Maybe you can learn a few things from our mistakes...

247

The Launderer

The laundry room was run by a shady guy who had a couple of Laundromats scattered around town. He was the kind of guy that made you feel a little dirty, you know? Jackie mentioned that she had met him before. Randomly, she was in one of his Laundromats, drying clothes, when he came out of his office, screaming at a woman – the woman was either a worker or his wife...not sure – about some laundry mishap. Jackie said it was horrible. My wife says that after giving the woman an earful, he turned to Jackie and asked for her opinion on the matter. She told him he was disgusting and that she would never be back.

So we had that to look forward to.

Our newly acquired laundry room had four washers and dryers. Even with that number, we'd only get a $100 cut from the Launderer. Given that the utilities were running at over $200 – to say nothing of the fact that some of the machines didn't run at all – we were losing some serious money on this gig. So I told the Launderer no thanks and sent him packing. Launderer out = good. The fact that we had to run the service on our own now = bad.

I ordered four new washers and dryers, which rang up a one time bill of almost $5,000. Maytag. Listen, reader, I don't care how many of those ridiculous Maytag commercials you've seen, there doesn't seem to be any such thing as a Maytag repairman.

The Launderers Lesson #1: Even if you've got someone to run your laundry room, expect about six pounds of headaches. You'll be repairing and replacing machines more often than will even seem possible.

So with our Maytag gear, we could never get a repairman over to the place. We couldn't even get replacement parts.

Tired of the corporate bullshit, I called a local repairman named Bud to see if he could help. Bud was about what you'd expect from a man named Bud, only fatter. Always with a cap on his head and a crack gleaming from behind. And despite the stereotypes associated with his name, he always seemed to be knowledgeable about washers and dryers.

Unfortunately, he turned out to be a scammer. A launderer of a different kind. I soon realized that he wasn't actually fixing my broken machines. He was just moving the working ones around with the broken ones and then claiming he'd fixed them. Then, when the formerly "working" ones turned up broken, he'd come in and bill me again. Nice racket, that one. He claimed it was all just a mix-up, too.

Well, I sorted him out. I numbered all the machines and pulled them away from the wall so he wouldn't get "confused" again. The bills really piled up with this guy. He just kept "fixing" the same machine over and over again.

We never made a dime on the laundry room. Actually, let's make that one a lesson...

The **Launderers Lesson #2**: Don't expect to make a dime on your laundry room.

Lesson #2 was frustrating for us because the local repairmen would come out and bill for a repair without actually fixing anything. Didn't seem to matter who we called. When we got rid of Bud, some other phony in overalls ripped us off. When we got rid of him, it was the slick fatso with a Leatherman tool-belt. Seemed like we were calling repairmen all the time and they never fixed anything.

So I responded in the way I naturally respond to such things: I got a repair manual and started doing minor repairs myself. I remember telling Jackie that I didn't want to learn anything else about fixing stuff, my head had gotten so full of diagrams and schematics and part relationships.

The next step, then, was to pass the buck. We closed the laundry room and put washer and dryer hookups in the apartments. So now we can leave the laundry issue to the tenants – and they can worry about repairing their own washer/dryers. Plus, it meant a healthy raise in rent every time a new vacancy came up.

Oh, yeah, and also, it meant a drop in our electric bill. See, laundry rooms soak up a hell of a lot of power. When we got rid of those washers and dryers, our utility bill was literally cut in half.

Alright, I'm done with this section. It's frustrating to even write about. But one last thing. I just want to say this publicly...Screw you, Maytag repairman!

Okay. I feel better now.

The Pool Man

Let's move over about six feet from the laundry room and dialogue on my other massive migraine, shall we? Ah, the 30' x 50' swimming pool. A pool is like anything else that requires maintenance. At first, it's fun. I would take the boys with me whenever I had to clean the thing and they would play and harass me while I did the job. Seemed like I was always skimming the damn thing – mostly, I was...the pool was located next to a heavily wooded area, so I was always skimming the leaves from the large oak trees nearby. Every time the wind blew, or after a particularly heavy summer storm, I would have to race over to get the leaves out of the pool. See, some leaves you don't have to worry so much about, but oak leaves have a powerful acid in them; an acid that leaves a nice brown spot on the pool flooring.

As you can imagine, this chore got old quick. It was time-consuming and exhausting. And it wasn't the only chore, either. During the summer, I had to check on the pool more often because the sun would deplete the chlorine. I had read newspaper stories about a water park where kids got sick, so I became a bit paranoid about sanitation.

Then there was the pump. I installed a timer on the pump to save electricity, but eventually let it run continuously (more fear about sanitation). I later installed a chlorine feeder, which really helped alleviate my concerns (and my workload). I could fill it up twice a week and it would keep the pool straight.

The cleaning and the maintenance were tough, but not nearly as tough as the repair work. I learned the hard way how to replace the pumps and valve...

But let's not go there just yet. Let's talk about the little things first, then work our way toward the hernias. Most states have a law that pools have to be fenced in. So our pool was fenced in, complete with a swinging gate with a safety catch. With all the careless people going in and out of the pool on a daily basis, keeping this gate working and up to code was a real hassle. I installed all the required safety equipment, but users would invariably damage the safety ring and break the hooks.

But all the safety in the world won't prevent the most disturbing problem: unauthorized use of the pool. I'll get into this issue in a little more detail later, but for now, I'll need to mention it to justify a "fix" I had to implement. I would get home and get a call that some people had pulled up and dumped fifteen kids out at the pool. You would not believe how people will just show up like they own the place. I got so desperate to control use that I bought and assembled a metal roof and wall structure to put over the pool – so we now had an indoor pool. Brilliant idea.

Now that we had shade, even in the heat of the summer, the water would be 65 degrees. So I had to order and install a heater. The heating bill was around $300 a month. I could have lived with the cost, but in the mornings, the inside of the building would be dripping with condensation. Within a week, I had rust on all the exposed metal.

Okay, so now I needed a cover for the water. I tried to make a cover using polyurethane, but it sank to the bottom of the pool. It weighed about 800 pounds when the water was on top of it. When I finally got it out (I'm not even going to go into that ridiculous struggle) it was a jumbled mess. So then I broke down and got a store-bought cover. But once I'd opened the container, I realized that the cover alone wasn't enough. I also had to buy a reel system to deploy the cover.

So after I installed and secured everything – believe me, it was a full day's work – I was finally able to go home. The minute I got home, reader (the freaking *minute* I got home); I got a call from a concerned tenant regarding more unauthorized use.

So I returned to the complex. Again. There, I found at least fifteen bikes in a pile. The back door to my makeshift building had been kicked open (a foot mark on the "No Trespassing" sign). I opened the door to find fifteen little kids raising hell in the pool. The oldest among them was 12 or 13. It was kind of funny.

Trying to keep a straight face, I hollered, "Police! Up against the wall."

The kids jumped out of the pool and lined up against the wall. They were stiff as boards, shivering, and dripping from head to toe.

I got out my clipboard and walked past each one, taking down their names. One of them, as it turned out, was a local policeman's boy. I found out that the group had ridden two miles on their bikes to break in and swim. You know I was mad, reader, but I was also concerned. It's kind of terrifying to think that there wasn't anyone in the whole group old enough to take care of all these kids. It was a miracle that no one drowned or got hurt in their horseplay.

So that was it. I snapped on the whole pool agenda right then and there. Even though we'd dumped so much money into repairing and protecting the place, I just couldn't take it anymore.

So I asked Jackie to call the tenants and see if they would be willing to pay an extra $25 in rent for the pool. Nobody wanted to pay the extra. So I locked the pool building and drained it, never to open it again.

Unfortunately, my swimming pool troubles wouldn't end there. We obtained another pool and laundry room with our second 24-unit apartment complex. When I first looked at the pool, I noticed that it had one of the deepest deep ends I had ever seen. It was sixteen feet deep despite being the same length and width as our first inherited pool.

In the first season at this complex, we were in a "manage to own" agreement with the seller, so we couldn't make any significant changes. The repairs, however, remained squarely in our court.

Almost right after we signed our agreement, the owner told me that the bottom drain in the deep end of the pool was clogged and that I would need to do whatever it was I needed to do to unclog the bastard. I initially prepared the pool by pumping it out with a lagoon pump. Remembering my lessons from pool #1, I installed a chlorine feeder before I even got down to brass tacks. I'd find later that the feeder wouldn't be enough in this case. Even with it running at full blast, a green layer of gross would form in the bottom of the deep end.

Anyway, pool now mostly drained (with drains, you have to leave a little water behind); I could get down to the business of unclogging drains. I had a couple of augers on hand, so I tried to rotor the drain. I'd take a deep breath, dive down to the drain, and crank away. No luck.

When I went back to the building supply store for more supplies, I met a woman who worked for the rescue squad. She thought it would be fun to put on a wet suit and scuba dive in the pool. I guess she thought it might be good practice. So I stood on the deck and fed her some kind of metal tape to keep her breathing. She was determined to get that thing unstuck, but it was hopeless. I told her to forget it, gave her $100, and sent her on her way.

So I went back to Rental Service Corporation and rented the pump again. The pool now fully drained, I could walk around freely. I put the blade of the auger into the bottom drain. Immediately, it hit something and strained. After a bunch of grunting and grinding, it finally freed up and took off deeper into the pipe. I looked down to find that red builder sand was pumping out of the drain. I had drilled through the plastic pipe. Shit.

Because the deck was concrete, I had to rent a brick-saw to fix the mess. Now a brick-saw has a diamond blade and you hook a water hose up to it (the water cools the blade). This is an expensive piece of equipment. I spent the rest of the day sawing rectangles into the concrete deck.

When I was done, I returned the saw and got a pry bar and began working my blocks out of the deck. The first one was tough, but once I got it opened up, I could use the pry bar and shims and flip the blocks out onto the deck. I then would toss them onto a hand truck – kind of like a wheeled cart used to haul refrigerators. The blocks weighed over 400 pounds. As soon as I loaded up the last block, the cheep little wheels fell off the cart. I wonder if the Egyptians ever had to deal with this kind of bullshit.

The worst part was that once I got all this done, I felt along the outside shell of the pool, but could not find the pipe. I had an idea about where it should have been, but it was apparently deeper than I'd thought. So I slept on it, rented the saw again the next day, and removed more of the deck. I'd removed a rectangle about 5' x 25' by the time I finally found the pipe. I then exposed the pipe all the way down to the deep end of the pool, where it got too deep to reach.

Now I was in need of an excavator – think of a big steam shovel, only one that runs on gas – so I went back to Rental Service Corporation and took one out. It fit into the pool area, but couldn't reach the pit from the spot it could park. SMASH! I pulled down a section of the brick wall separating the excavator from the rim of the pool and drove onto the deck. I had a friend who knew how to run a backhoe help me. He excavated a 15-foot hole, but still no pipe.

I sat down for a while, frustrated as all hell, before walking to Jacks to buy a large Coke. While enjoying my beverage, I had an epiphany: I could run some water backward from the pump and maybe reveal the leak that way.

So I went back to the pool and put a hose in the pipe, letting the water fly. I was standing by the huge hole, waiting for some sign, any sign, but nothing happened at first. Suddenly, the red dirt started to avalanche down the side of the exposed pool shell. When it was done, a vision: there was the pipe! I let the water run until I could see the entire pipe. It was only two feet underground, but was blocked at a 45 degree fitting. We missed the pipe on the first tries because it hugged the curve of the pool's side.

Reinvigorated, I threw down the Coke and ran for my hack-saw. Without wasting any time, I sawed the pipe. It would be an understatement to say that I was shocked by what I found. It was about quitting time and I was sunburned and exhausted, so I thought maybe I was hallucinating.

I called Jackie, who was playing golf in a mixed scramble tournament. "Guess what?" I said excitedly. "I found the blockage in the swimming pool...it's a Jack Nicholas autographed golf ball."

My wife about choked as she took a sip of her beer. Talk about ironic. Jackie's out playing golf while I'm the one digging around for a golf ball. I hate golf – or at least I do now that damn ball caused me so much trouble. We still have it, though. A monument to my labors, I guess. And, hell, maybe it's worth some decent money.

I managed to fill in the hole in a hurry that day. The form for the concrete repair was already there. The deck looked like a giant puzzle with a section missing. So I ordered three yards of cement and got everything patched up. I even hired some kids from the local school to help take care of the pool while the concrete dried. Before I left, I used my finger to write Jackie and the boys' names in the new slab. I then added the date and drew a heart around the whole thing. Well, it was my pool, after all! I could do whatever I damn well wanted with it.

I cleaned the dirt out of the pool, climbed in my truck, and headed home. It was beautiful that day. When I arrived home, the boys were in batman costumes, jumping on the trampoline, our two Labradors sitting nearby, just to make sure they didn't fall. The grill was fired and Jackie came out of the kitchen with two Bud Lights. She handed me one and told me how much fun she'd had in the golf tournament. We sat down and she asked me about the job at the pool. I sipped my beer and smiled as we watched the sun go down. It would be several days before I told her the whole ordeal.

I know I went into great detail about the pool repair, but this is one of those stories that might help you save a ton of money. It would have cost at least $5,000 to $20,000 to hire a professional plumber to fix the pool. I spent about $400 in equipment rentals and $200 for concrete. In the end, you have to look for opportunities like these. It's the only way to get by.

Now let's shift gears and talk about hiring someone to manage your pool.

I hired the same two boys from the local school to do standby maintenance for me. I showed them how to check the pool and told them to be available for calls. I paid them in advance and gave them another $100 for emergency maintenance expenses.

Never leave young boys with loads of cash.

When I returned to the complex, I could have popped them both. They had used the $100 to buy booze! They were so drunk that I couldn't possibly allow them to leave the premises. They thought this was so funny, but I was very disappointed and knew I couldn't trust them again.

So it was back to the drawing board on that one. And I turned to the place that I always turned to for help: myself.

My schedule allowed me to do maintenance in the middle of the day, so I'd be able to clean the pool on my own. Being out there every day gave me a sunburn. Plus, when the pool was drained, I used muriatic acid, which takes your breath away, but cleans really well. In addition to that, I would have to repaint the pool on a yearly basis. Whenever I painted, I would do the deep end in the morning, and by the time the sun was on the other side of the horizon, the pool would reflect its rays from all sides. It always felt like I was in a microwave. A few times, I thought I had heat stroke.

Whenever I finished putting the pretty blue paint on the pool, I would try to stick it out to make sure it dried, but one year, I felt so bad from the heat that I went home to rest. After a couple of hours, I drove back to check on my work and discovered that a kid had climbed the fence and ridden his skateboard all over the pretty blue wall, which was now covered with black rubber skid marks. If I hadn't had heat stroke earlier, I was ready for it now. I felt utterly defeated.

The next morning, I was back at it. I put another coat of paint over the wall and stayed around until it dried. I filled the pool before I left, just to make sure it couldn't be vandalized again. The little jerk left his skateboard in the back of the building. I knew who it belonged to, but when I asked him about it, he didn't claim it. So I dumped the skateboard into the 9-yard garbage dumpster out back.

So we've done daily maintenance, significant repairs, and yearly maintenance. Let's talk a little more about policing a swimming pool.

Random people just wandering up and jumping in...that was a constant problem. At first, I simply told the people I didn't know to leave and not come back or I would have them arrested. That didn't work at all. They would drag ass around and finally leave, but would always come back. The kind of person who crashes a pool also happens to be the kind of person not afraid of the police, I guess. Or maybe they just like the meals they serve in jail. I don't know.

When the issues started getting really out of control, I finally said, "Screw it," and changed my approach. One afternoon, I saw a thug I didn't recognize swimming in the pool. So I walked up and introduced myself and told him that I needed to collect his swimming fee. Just got a dumb look back. I told him the swimming fee was $5 a day. He apologized, saying he didn't know that this was a private pool and left. After word got out that the swimming fee was $5, the trespassers stopped coming. Seriously. Threatening legal action didn't stop them. Five bones did. I guess I was getting into their beer money or something – and you know that wasn't going to fly.

Now, not all non-tenant pool users are difficult. In fact, you can use them as a nice little side-line to make money…

For instance, we had a nice family from the adjacent neighborhood pay $150 a summer to use the pool for a private birthday party. Enjoying the extra cash, we decided to start a little pool club. The funds from that enterprise paid for a lot of the chlorine. You might think that one might have to worry about liability by accepting money from non-tenants, but I found that it didn't make a difference legally. And besides, it put an end to the problem of trespassing.

It would be a short-lived bit of success, though, as we did this for only two summers. We just couldn't take the maintenance and constant need for monitoring anymore.

Here's when the wave finally broke and rolled back for me:

Some of our tenants didn't watch their kids. I mean really small kids would climb the wall and sit on top, looking down at the people in the pool. One day, I knocked on the door that I knew belonged to one of the kids' mothers. When she answered, I begged her, "Please don't let your child climb and sit on the wall. He must be supervised if he's outside...especially around the pool."

The mother just rolled her eyes and said, "He ain't swimming. He don't know how to swim."

I just stared at her for a minute, unable to believe just how stupid she seemed to be. I thanked her nonetheless before walking back to the wall and putting the little guy on the ground. He followed me back to his apartment, where I said to his mother, "Here's your baby. The pool is closed."

When the last person left that afternoon, I went to the pump room and drained the pool. It was never opened again.

Whether it's a motel or an apartment complex, everyone says they want a pool. But despite all the effort, probably 95% of our tenants never even used the pool. Meanwhile, during the summer, the pool caused problems in one way or another for 100% of the tenants. And it caused us great stress.

So here's our bottom line and our only lesson for the **Pool Man section – Lesson #1**: Swimming pools are a huge pain in the ass.

The (Creepy and Lazy) Resident Manager

In the course of my police career, I met a Navy guy named Arnold. Arnold was smart, interesting, and good with computers, so when his enlistment was up, I thought he might make a good on-site manager at one of our apartment complexes. I offered him a rent-free apartment in exchange for his managing services. He thought it was a great deal and agreed. I gave him the keys to the washing machines so he could also keep them clean and roll the quarters for Jackie's deposit.

The first month, Arnold handed me a twenty dollar bill and said he had used some of the quarters from the laundry room to go to the local bar. The second month, he handed Jackie $80 in rolled quarters. This was pretty clear evidence that he was stealing because my wife had always taken about $400 to the bank every month before.

"You should get the keys back from him," she said. "He's stealing from us."

So I did what a good husband should: I listened to my wife. I knocked on Arnold's door and told him I needed the keys to work on the machines. When he handed over the keys, I went over to the laundry room and pretended to work on the machines, but then I never gave those keys back. The next day, he asked for them back, but I told him that

Jackie had decided that she enjoyed rolling the quarters and that she was going to do it from now on. From that month forward, the deposits were back to $400 a month.

Arnold might have been our first resident manager, but I had watched other companies struggle with them, as well. They started out okay, but as time goes on, their service deteriorates.

For example, at first, Arnold helped me get the pool in order, so I felt like his services were worth a couple of hundred dollars towards the rent. But then, every month, he got lazier and grew fatter.

Case and point: one of my peeves was always trash on the ground. At a complex, trash needs to be picked up at least once a week. I'm talking about picking up maybe ten pieces of trash – not a big job. But with Arnold under our employ, whenever I was on the property, I would constantly have to bend over to pick up cans and trash.

I remember when the trash issue finally reached its breaking point. I would say to him, "There's paper on the sidewalk. Make sure you clean it up on your way out."

"Sure," he would say. And then I would watch him leave. He would step right over the piece of paper as he walked to his car. I couldn't believe it. I mean, how lazy can you be? He had to *step over it*.

Finally, I told him that I wanted to talk to him. He wanted to talk on the sidewalk, but I told him that we needed to speak privately. We agreed on a time that would work for the two of us, along with Jackie.

When the time of the meeting came, my wife and I did our best to look stern and final.

"Look," I said. "This isn't working out. You aren't keeping the place neat enough."

"Oh yeah," he said, starting in with me. "I was just going to pick up that piece of notebook paper." So he knew exactly what I was talking about.

I raised a hand to cut him off. "It's too late," I told him. "I hired you to take the stress off of me, but since you've been here, my stress level has actually *increased*."

No one likes to get fired, and Arnold was no exception. I could tell he was getting mad. I told him he could stay in the apartment and pay rent, but that I could no longer afford to give him a free place. He was shaken up and told us he would think it over and give us an answer on the following day. He wound up staying in the apartment for only $250 a month.

Arnold had a great job at an electric company, but after the initial month, it became increasingly difficult to collect the rent. I had to go to his workplace and hunt him down. He always had an excuse.

"I went home for Christmas and a friend wanted to buy a car for fifteen-thousand," he would say. "He didn't have good credit, so I co-signed and now my check is being garnished."

That was a new one. I thought that was a strange story. Between that and the stealing, this guy was beginning to look a little shady. Jackie said something was wrong with him (more on this later) and that he smelled funny. I told her that he was just a bachelor and had led a hard life. But my wife wasn't buying it.

"I want him gone," she said. I guess she'd gotten to the point where she couldn't even stand looking at him. "He makes the hair on the back of my neck stand up just thinking about him."

So once again, I did what a good husband should. I convinced Arnold to move out. To his credit, he agreed. By the end of the conversation, he actually seemed to think that it was his idea to leave.

So the bottom line is, even when you hire a manager (a person of supposed authority), you can't forget that you still have to manage your managers. It sounds a bit ridiculous, doesn't it? But, you can't expect everyone you hire to do things exactly the way you would have, just like you can't expect your tenants to be perfect little angels.

Chapter Ten

Dealing with Apartment Complex Tenants

Here's a one-liner for you, reader: When you first meet a prospective tenant, it's a little like going on a first date. You make eye contact, they usually flirt with you for a cheaper rate, and you only get to know each other briefly before you decide on the second date – that being the day they move in. And just like dating, no matter how selective you are, you wind up spending more of your time with a loser or two than you might like.

Bad Tenants (The Ones You Never See Coming)

Being that we were all well-to-do with our apartment complex now, we began renting out our vacant units to the kinds of people you would expect to be excellent tenants. You can imagine where this is going before it even starts: you shouldn't judge a book by its cover, reader. Except maybe for this book, which in my humble opinion, has an excellent cover.

The Cop

Our first unexpectedly horrible tenant was a man named Michael. Given that he was a well-spoken police officer, I figured he would be a comfort to our tenants (to say nothing of Jackie and me). And since I had worked in law enforcement, I knew that Michael couldn't help but have a clean background – the agencies do extensive background checks before hiring anyone. Plus, he had a wife and family. They even seemed *nice*.

One day, I was at a local gas station where one of our tenants worked – there to pick up a rent check, if memory serves. This tenant was friendly, if not a bit of a liar, and had two daughters around thirteen and fourteen years old. Let's call her Jessie, the mother. Anyway, I was surprised to see Michael there (what a coincidence, right?), but more surprised to see him openly flirting with one of the young daughters. The daughter flirted right back, but c'mon. I guess her mother noticed how appalled I was by the whole scene, because she eventually turned to her daughter and told her to stop "harassing the policeman."

I remember that Michael was standing very close to the little girl when he replied, "Ah, she isn't bothering me." He was standing so close that the girl could probably feel his breath rush through her hair.

Now Jessie was divorced and had enjoyed a string of loser boyfriends. She had just met a guy from Mexico at church, who moved in with her almost immediately. But that's beside the point. The point is that, looking at Michael and Jessie's young daughter, it struck me that this policeman was as old as me, but was still throwing a pretty aggressive game. It looked entirely possible that he felt he could get in with this girl – the stupid grin on his face said as much. The worst part was that I knew that Jessie didn't have enough sense to recognize the possibility of trouble. She had been married to a policeman, after all, so she probably hoped that her daughter would marry one, too.

I just left, shaking my head.

It wasn't long after this that we received a call from Michael's neighbor; he was beating his wife. Quickly,

Jackie and I went to the apartment complex. Of course the neighbor called to complain well after the fact, so by the time we arrived, policeman and wife were gone. I did find that the door had been kicked in, though, so I repaired it and left a note, hoping to set up a meeting with the two of them. When I received no response, I stopped by the apartment to find the telltale signs of a move-out. It was obvious no one was living there.

I called the police department and left a message for Michael to call me. The detective said that Michael had been terminated for pawning a video camera.

"What's wrong with pawning a video camera?" I asked.

"It was his squad car video camera and recorder," the officer said, serious as the plague.

So the bonehead not only stole and pawned his own squad car's video camera, he pawned it in the *same town he worked in*! You can't make this shit up. So obviously, Michael got caught when the pawn dealer called the detective and the detective checked it out.

When the detective arrived at the pawn shop, he found that the camera still had the State of Alabama numbers on it.

Michael immediately turned in his resignation in hopes of not being prosecuted. He left Alabama, moving about 45 minutes away to Hattisburg, Mississippi. The following weekend, I ran into him at Books-A-Million, where I convinced him to get the rest of his things out of the unit by the following weekend. To my delight, he did show up that weekend. His poor wife helped him load the truck. I felt sorry for her and their child. Anyone stupid enough to do what he did with his video camera is certainly possessed of an ignorance nothing short of dangerous.

In future, I was occasionally approached by police officers looking for free apartments. I guess they figured they could capitalize on their jobs by offering protection for the tenants in exchange for a free place to stay. They weren't just getting this idea out of the sky, either. At the time, the housing projects in the area were allowing police to stay rent-free. I remember talking to the manager of the Crossgate Housing Project. She told me that they had to kick their police guy out because he wouldn't do anything. He let beer parties and drug deals go on right in the parking lot and never helped at all. So whenever cops came knocking, I shunned away, saying we couldn't afford to have an empty or non-paying unit.

The Truck Drivers

Some of our biggest rent dodgers (and womanizers) were truck drivers. I guess this was just an ideal job for debt dodgers because their wages were excellent and a person with a good driver's license could work anywhere in the country. They would work out of state for a truck-driving line. The minute the courts started to garnish their wages, they would shoot across the state line to another agency.

It was easy for them because they made plenty of contacts with the other agencies when moving trailers. It was also easy for them to get a good reference from these same agencies. I would call them up to verify employment and would be given a positive reference almost every time. After all, their jobs required them to drive trailers full of thousands of dollars of merchandise, toxic fuel, and other dangerous material – *of course* they would be trustworthy to send in the rent.

One day, I spoke with a lady at a major truck line about an applicant, telling her I was concerned because of the short amount of time he had worked for them. She explained to me that it was typical for drivers to move from one agency to another because the driver could get work anywhere he wanted. Still, she didn't think this particular applicant would have any problem paying rent. Most of these guys were clearing four or five thousand dollars a month, but it almost seemed to me that the truck transport companies were helping these truckers dodge their responsibilities.

I was working on an apartment when a fat-bellied trucker named Cedric Taylor drove up. He was an arrogant guy who needed an apartment for his girlfriend. I verified his job and income with the major trucking line he worked for. It was just like I mentioned above – he had bounced around from company to company, but they all gave him a good report.

His girlfriend, meanwhile, was named Shaquikwa. I knew Cedric would probably ditch her in this apartment, so I told him he'd have to pay a $900 deposit up front. I figured that would cover our expenses, should she not be able to pay the rent.

As it turned out, Shaquikwa was sick with a blood disease and got almost $1,700 a month in welfare. She had a sweet little boy named Luis who also happened to be a little slow. But he was friendly as you can imagine and would run around on the sidewalks, talking to everyone. As he grew older, he became a nuisance – but that's beside the point.

Anyway, Shaquikwa was in and out of the hospital. When not in the hospital, she was in bed, sick. Despite these illnesses, she always managed to have different men in her apartment.

One day, Shaquikwa was furious, so she told us that Cedric was married and was actually having an affair with her.

Thank goodness we collected the larger deposit, because here is where the ditching comes in to play. I asked Cedric about Shaquikwa's accusations and he admitted that he had problems with women and that his wife wanted him back. His face was priceless when he told me that. I guess he thought he was some kind of precious player, but in reality, he was a short, fat, bald guy. Definitely not the Romeo he saw when he looked in the mirror. Talk about distorted body image.

Construction Workers

Jackie got a call from a local construction company entrenched in the construction of the new prison. The company wanted to lease an apartment for a couple of their workers they had assigned to the project. Jackie took the lease to the company and had the foreman sign it. We didn't even think twice about it, figuring that we were dealing with a reputable company that could be counted on for the rent.

What we didn't figure was the caliber of the workers who would be staying with us. The company brought people in from all over the state. Most of these workers were plumbers who would work a week or two and then go home. A lot of them seemed like crackheads (or at least part time crackheads). I first got suspicious when I caught a local crackhead we all called "Happy Britches" (more on why that is later) visiting the workers in their unit. There was just no legitimate reason for this guy to be visiting a bunch of plumbers unless he was hustling up crack for them.

So I went up to one of the plumbers one day. "That guy...that Happy Britches," I said to him. "He's been ordered by the courts to stay off our property." Again, more on that story later.

"Oh, I'm sorry," the plumber said, seeming unable to look me in the eye. "I didn't know."

I tried to catch his line of sight. "There is no legitimate reason for that guy to be here," I said. "If he shows up again, I'll have the police remove him from the property. And I can't be responsible for what they find when they bust in."

The worker blinked. There was no doubt in my mind what Happy Britches was providing. So I had a unit full of plumbers by day, crackheads by night.

The Mormons

I guess you've probably seen the young men riding bikes. They wear dress pants and white shirts with black shoes. They travel door to door at the most inconvenient times, wanting to talk about Jesus. Well, these guys are called elders and they work for the Mormons. I actually had the opportunity to rent to four of these guys, which was nice for a while because their church paid the rent to me faithfully on the first of every month.

Dealing with Apartment Complex Tenants Lesson #1: If somebody has to sign their lease under the name of God, expect to get screwed. God doesn't write checks.

I remember trying to talk to one of them one day. I asked him what his name was and told me it was "Elder."

"No," I said. "I mean your real name."

"Elder," he said, serious as a heart attack.

I ended the conversation because if the creepy kid wasn't going to give me his real name, I wasn't going to waste my breath trying to be friendly.

You know, when you see these guys riding around on their bikes, it looks aimless, but in fact it is not. I can say this with certainty because they had bulletin boards and maps of the city posted in their apartment. They used the boards to divvy up grids for each elder to canvass. It looked like a command center. There was nothing innocent or aimless about the way they worked the community.

Later, we rented an apartment to a Mormon couple named Williams. Mr. Williams and his wife worked for the same church that the kids with the command center studied under. Only this time, the elder of the church didn't sign the lease for our tenants.

One day, Mr. Williams called about a repair to be made in his bathroom. I was working on the bathtub and he was standing right over me. He was one of those guys who would get on your nerves. Jackie and I cringed whenever he or his wife would try to talk to us. I got so tired of his mouth that I planned my stops when I knew he wouldn't be home.

After talking to him one time, I got the impression that he and his wife were using the church as a means to travel. He listed three different cities he had stayed in during the previous six months. I got the idea that they were just passing through, despite the fact they had signed a one-year lease. Sure enough, he called after three months, wanting to get out of the lease. Jackie told him he was responsible for payment of rent for one year. She told him once he was out that we would try to rent the unit, but that he was ultimately responsible for payment as long as it was vacant.

We actually rented the apartment around the 20th of the following month. So he called us and said he wanted his prorated rent back, plus his deposit. He sent a threatening letter to us about how he was going to contact the attorney general – a letter that really got Jackie upset.

My reply stated that he owed us for the remaining nine months on the lease, and that he had used us as a short-term place to stay with no intention of fulfilling said lease. "Just because you've crossed state lines," my letter said, "that doesn't mean we won't pursue what we are owed." I went on to promise him that if he ever returned to Alabama, I would have papers served on him and would sue for the full amount of damages as specified by our contract.

Elder Williams never wrote or called again. I was glad to be rid of that manipulative, creepy, old bible-banger.

The Immigrants

During the late 90's, D experienced an influx of people from Mexico. So we found that many of our new applicants were Mexican.

We rented an apartment to one such woman named Maria. She brought along her two boys. She had been referred to us by a successful local businessman originally from Honduras. I guess he was helping her because she was trying to leave an abusive relationship.

Maria worked at one of the food processing plants and made enough money to afford the apartment. We got her settled into a unit and she paid her rent on time every month. One of her boys was an adult and spoke a little English, but her other son, Juan, was seven and spoke English very well.

It wasn't even a week after they got settled that we received a call about finding an apartment for Maria's uncle and his wife. Her uncle was a gray-haired old fellow who also worked at the processing plant. They rented an apartment in the same complex as Maria and her boys and lived quietly by themselves. They were great tenants.

After a month, everything was fine with all these tenants. And then we added another Mexican family when Juan called to ask about an apartment for his aunt. I don't have much in the way of impressions of these two, save for the fact that the aunt was a beautiful woman and her husband was tall. They didn't speak much English, but we still managed to communicate with them to collect the rent. All three families shared the same sidewalk and seemed to be happy in each other's company. Jackie and I developed a pretty high opinion of our Mexican tenants because they seemed very hard-working and paid the rent promptly.

After working with and getting to know our Mexican tenants, their friends and extended families, I began to think that there were a few differences between the ones that came through Texas and the ones that came through California. The ones who traveled from Texas typically wore cowboy hats and were very polite. The ones who traveled through California wore trendy clothes, bandanas, and jewelry. One of the kids from California had what I would call a "gangster" look. He did his hair with mousse, wore flashy "bling," and listened to the most violent rap music.

One of the Mexicans from California had a baby with a local girl named Tameka. She was fresh from the country where she lived in a shack without running water. I first met her when she called to complain about her boyfriend, Jose, who was living with her uncle. She called the police and told them her boyfriend was illegal. Of course, he disappeared, but I was still worried that she would stir up enough mess to scare off our rent-paying, quiet Mexican tenants.

I went to the apartment to meet with Tameka after she called the police. She was a tall woman around twenty years old. After speaking with her, I realized that she was mentally challenged. She couldn't speak any Spanish and her boyfriend, who was now her baby daddy could not speak English.

I tried to settle her down about Jose.

"Look, Tameka," I said. "If you call the police on Jose, they will take him to Mexico and your baby will never know his daddy."

"Oh," she said. "I don't want him to be taken away. I just wanted him to take us to McDonald's."

I told her that if she kept bugging the police about nonsense, she and Jose would have to move out of the complex.

Jackie rented a unit on the other side of the complex to a Mexican woman named Tammy who had two daughters. One was in her early twenties and the other was around fourteen. The girls had a California feel about them and spoke like they were from the ghetto. Tammy, meanwhile, was kind of a mystery. She managed to pay her rent, but it seemed like she left her daughters alone for long periods of time.

One night, I got a call from a tenant in the unit adjacent to Tammy's. She was complaining about water coming into her kitchen. Jackie and I hustled over and realized the water was coming from Tammy's unit.

We knocked on Tammy's door until the fourteen-year-old finally opened it.

"Here to check on a leak," I said. When I got to their living room, my heart sank. The floor was soaked. A puddle had collected near the wall and seemed to be draining into the kitchen, both under the door and *through the wall*. I walked over to the bathroom to find the problem: the shutoff valve for the toilet. I stopped up the water and replaced the valve. Thank goodness it was easy to fix.

But where was there mother? The wall was so damaged that the water had to have been running for two weeks or more. And *no one had called.* Jackie investigated and found out that Tammy was in Mexico and had left her two daughters alone. Only trouble was that the older daughter had moved in with a kid that often waited on us at La Palacia. The younger girl must have been by herself for weeks.

We later rented a unit to Joey, who worked for Steel Disposal, the local garbage collection company. He was a pretty good tenant as far as paying his rent. The problem we had with him was his friends. He evidently knew a bunch of street people that he loved to drink and play cards with. The worst of the group were the ones that drove a green, 4-door Cougar with tinted windows. They were classy enough to have been evicted from a trailer they rented.

One night, I received a call from Miguel (a seven-year-old who lived in the complex) that there had been a stabbing. I prodded Miguel for details, but he didn't know the whole story. Evidently, a policeman had already arrived on the scene and gotten medical treatment for the victim, one of our tenants from Mexico. From what I understood, he was having trouble getting to the bottom the story, too.

It would be a few hours before we could piece it all together. Here's how it went:

The victim was walking home to his apartment when he passed the green Cougar. The two men in the Cougar jumped out, roughed him up, and demanded his money. When my tenant wouldn't give it to them, they stabbed him and took off.

Since I knew the description of the car matched that of Joey's friends, I asked him about it. He said he didn't know anything about the stabbing.

"Fine, then," I said skeptically. "Just make sure those guys and whoever else rides around in that Cougar that they're no longer allowed on the property."

He nodded blankly, so I added a little emphasis.

"I never want to see that car parked anywhere on my property again, you understand?"

He nodded again. More emphatically this time.

Joey looked afraid, but to his credit, I never saw that car again at the complex. Once the legal issues all shook down, it turned out that the primary drivers of the car were Joey's girlfriend and her friend, both career criminals. The reason it took so long to get to the bottom of things was that the victim was an illegal immigrant and didn't want to talk to the police. I guess this is what made my tenant a particularly inviting victim. In fact, I've heard that it happens a lot in bigger cities – thugs pulling robberies on aliens because they won't report anything to the cops for fear of being deported.

Joey also felt terrible. He wanted me to escort him down to the apartment complex to see the man who had been stabbed. So I did.

When we got there, I asked the victim if Joey had been the guy that stabbed him.

"No," he said, sounding certain.

My tenant then looked back at his friends and family and said (seriously), "Don't kill this one."

You have to hand it to the Mexicans. They might not have been much for reporting to the police, but they sure took care of their own business.

By this time, we had twenty-five Mexican immigrants living in five units of our apartment complex. We never once had any direct problems from any of them. Jackie and I really liked them all. One thing that I thought was neat was when they would string things along the ceiling. Instead of buying a floor lamp for the living room, they would staple extension cords to the walls and string lights along it – just like Christmas lights, but with regular light bulbs in the sockets. One guy ran strings up the wall and across the ceiling and down to the wall switch for the ceiling light. He had rigged little pulleys and could lie in bed and pull the cord and it would push the switch up or down to control the light.

While we were eating dinner, the owner of the local Mexican restaurant, Curly, approached our table and asked us if we had an apartment for rent for a man who worked for another business Curly owned.

We said, "Sure," so he introduced us to Anand, a man from Pakistan. We told the both of them about a one-bedroom apartment we had available.

Anand liked the apartment, so Curly signed the lease for him and he moved in. For the first few months, he paid on time. And then he started working in Huntsville. When he quit working for Curly, we let him sign his own lease because, by this time, he had established his own checking account.

The day he signed the lease, he had a girl named Lisa with him, but she didn't sign anything. About two weeks later, Lisa called Jackie because she wanted to get off the lease.

"But your name's not on the lease," Jackie told her.

A few minutes later, Lisa's father called. "I want to know whether my daughter has any liability on that apartment of yours," he said.

"No," Jackie said. "As I told your daughter, her name is not on the lease."

It was very confusing. Later, we learned what the trouble was: it seems that Anand had promised to pay Lisa if she would marry him. This way, he could get American citizenship. I guess he didn't pay, so the deal was off.

Citizen or no, Anand continued to rent from us. But after the Lisa incident, he was always late with the rent. One time, we even had to drive all the way to Tuscaloosa to look for him. I remember my ass-kicking wife picking up the cell phone and letting Anand in on the score.

"You're late on your rent again, Anand," she said.

"Oh, I know, Jackie," Anand said apologetically. "I've got the money for you. I just won't be back in Hasselville until next week."

"That's great!" Jackie said. "Because we're actually here in Huntsville right now. We'll be right over to pick it up."

Reluctantly, he agreed to bring it to us. It was a long time waiting in that Lowe's parking lot for him to bring the check. But he eventually did. By the end, it was a hassle to collect from him because he wasn't really living in the unit anymore.

Dealing with Apartment Complex Tenants Lesson #2: It might seem like a blessing if your tenants are never around, but trust me: if they aren't in the unit at least three weeks out of the month, they're probably planning to stiff you.

We were glad when Anand finally turned in his thirty-day notice and cleared the apartment. About five days after he moved out, though, he called Jackie and asked for a copy of his lease.

"Sure, Anand," Jackie said.

"Can I get one with Lisa's name on it?" he asked.

Jackie said she remembers pausing for a long time, confused. "Yours is the only name on the lease," she explained. "I'm not going to falsely add a new name to the contract."

We never heard from him again.

Problems with Teens

Let's talk about that old laundry room again for a minute. It's got a nice little story about what bastards teenage boys can be, anyway. Unlike our other properties, this laundry room featured a post office, complete with lock boxes. When we bought the place, only ten of the twenty-four boxes had working locks, so I ordered new locks from Home Depot.

As a little aside: you cannot imagine how much trouble people had keeping up with their mailbox keys. Every week, I would have to replace a lock or make another key. Someone would always holler at me just as I was calling it a day, too. "Hey Patrick, I can't find my mailbox key." It got to where I was hearing that statement in my sleep. I mean, it was only a five minute job, but it always seemed to happen when I was trying to do something else.

On my latest version of this ridiculously frequent job, I was just about to replace all the locks with non-locking snap doors when Jackie walked into the laundry room and told me that she had just received a call from the Joneses. A new box of checks had been stolen from their mailbox. One of the tenants' boys, Marty, had broken into the mailroom and stolen the checks. How do I know it was Marty? The genius used the checkbook to order Domino's Pizza to be delivered to his place. The check had bounced. So this crime was wrapped up fairly quickly. And his mother assured us that it would not happen again. Bonus.

After that little incident, I added a deadbolt lock to the mailroom door and made sure the postman had a key for access. Marty's mother begged Jackie to let her and Marty stay; assuring us that he would be supervised in the future. Jackie talked to the Joneses, who were very forgiving about the whole matter – boys will be boys, and all that. So we let them stay...a decision we would soon regret...

Problems with Teens Lesson #1: If you have a teen who causes a problem, it's likely because his/her parent(s) aren't willing or able to police their actions. You can warn both teen and parent, but don't expect any kind of miraculous turnaround. Sometimes, it's best to just cut them loose.

Marty was tall for his age, thin, and articulate, with a beautiful smile. He was always very respectful when he told us his absolute lies. He proved to be a thug of the highest order. He made friends with a child that lived in another unit and spent a lot of time over there with them. One day, while no one was home, he crawled into the neighbor's kitchen window and stole a cell phone belonging to Tulula, the mother of his friend.

Tulula called me right away and told me someone had broken into her apartment and that her cell phone was missing. I told her to call the police and that I was on my way. She got online to check her cell number and discovered a couple of calls were made to Domino's Pizza. Yes, Marty had ordered pizza and had it delivered once again to his apartment.

Jackie called the cell phone number and a girl answered. When my wife told her who she was, the girl panicked and hung up. The police went to Marty's apartment and arrested him again.

The next day, Marty's mother turned in the cell phone, saying she had fished it out of the dumpster, where Marty had admitted to throwing it. It did look pretty banged up and gross, that cell phone. It was an unfortunate situation they had going on in that unit. Marty's mom had a decent job, but she worked out of town – so her oldest daughter was supposed to be supervising Marty (this was the girl who answered when Jackie called the cell phone...she claimed she didn't know the phone was stolen).

I felt bad about it, but I knew I had to have the "Finished Business" talk with Marty's mom. More on that later.

As soon as I left, Marty's mom called Jackie, crying and begging her to let them stay. Jackie told her that we had to end the business because Marty was out of control and presented a danger to all the other tenants. The frantic mother finally got the message and was willing to cooperate. She called later that day and told Jackie that she would leave and go live with her aunt.

Jackie and I went to the U-Haul station, paid for a rental truck, and helped Marty's mom load up all their belongings. We then helped her unload her stuff into a mini storage unit. When we'd finished, Jackie wrote her a check for her deposit and wished her luck.

I'm sure my wife and I celebrated that night.

The following day was a Friday. I was making my usual rounds at the apartment complex (it's good to do this on weekend nights, just to ensure that things are quiet...check to make sure that no one is naked, standing on a retaining wall, and peeing, for example – we'll get to that little doozy later). Anyway, on that particular Friday, I walked by the unit where Marty and his mother used to live because I had noticed from the parking lot that the door was unlocked. I opened the door and found his mother. She was on the living room floor, bear assed and screwing some guy on the carpet. Empty beer cans were scattered on the floor all around them.

I quickly backed out, my arms raised.

Marty's mom got it together and came to the door. "Oh hey," she said, real coy-like. "I was just using the apartment for the weekend, trying to get my money's worth out of it, you know?"

I didn't even try to explain to her that she didn't live there anymore. I was still too weirded out by what I'd just seen. So I said, "Well, lock up when you're finished."

You know she had grown children. She had to be fifty-something. But you would've thought she was some little high school girl making out with her boyfriend. Any dark place she could find, I guess.

The whole thing made me feel really sorry for Marty. With no mother around – ever – he didn't really have much of a chance. Yep, I hated the little shit and felt sorry for him at the same time. It's strange, this business.

Like any business, it's one that plays with your emotions. It's always tough to find a balance between apathy and empathy. You want so much to trust everyone around you, but you still have to play the role of authority. Marty was one of the tough ones, but no matter how awful I felt about this *one* kid, I knew it wouldn't be the last time I experienced this kind of thing.

Chapter Eleven

Some Things Never Change

When we moved on up to the apartment complexes, Jackie and I figured that we would be able to kiss goodbye a few of the crime- and sex-related issues we were having with our low-income tenants. At least, we could focus more of our energy and attention on the type of tenant who wouldn't break the law. Or at least the type who would never be caught getting busy in public.

Boy were we wrong.

Make no mistake, reader. No matter where you are in the scale of things, land lording just comes with a few ingrained headaches. "Ingrained migraines" is maybe a better way to put it. Regardless of income, there is no escaping human nature. What's that they say? You can take the tenant out of the trailer park, but you can't take the trailer park out of the tenant...

The Dealers (Revisited)

Some time later, Jackie received a call from a young girl who had recently been hired at the public school in the next county. Adrian was her name. She was from the Dadson's Mill area, which at one time was so underdeveloped that it was basically just one little store on a crossroads. But in the seventies, over a hundred Section 8 project houses were built there, and the area quickly became a center for drugs and violence. Lacking any true police presence, the Dadson's Mill area had spawned some of the largest drug cartels ever seen in West Alabama.

Adrian was very well spoken and polite. She didn't have any credit, but she had just finished school and landed a good job, so we knew she could pay the rent. We were honestly proud of her. Proud. Pretty, young, and ambitious – we figured she would be a great tenant and blend in well with the other teachers and nurses living at the complex.

When I dropped by for some routine maintenance, I noticed that she was slowly but surely making her apartment a home. Gradually, the place was becoming nicely decorated and furnished.

She paid her rent on time and we had no problems with her. At first.

The Dealers (Revisited) Lesson #1: Even the people you least expect might turn out to be dealers. In fact, if you look at things from a dealer's perspective, the more levelheaded and honest you appear to be in your public life, the better.

One morning, a detective called and explained to me that a group of men were using Adrian's apartment to lay up during the day. Then, at night, they were selling marijuana in the projects. He said the main culprit was a notorious drug dealer from Dadson's Mills. I thanked him for the information. I was due to change air filters, anyway, so I thought I would start with her unit. You know, do a little snooping around.

From the moment I entered the unit, it was clear I was on to something. I could smell marijuana everywhere. I know what you're thinking, reader. Suffice to say, I know what weed smells like from my time as a conservation officer. Anyway, I also found other things: A half-consumed beer on the table, empties scattered on the floor, burn marks all over the carpet. It looked like someone was doing a lot of smoking. There was a large ash tray in the middle of the floor, full of half-burned joints, ashes, and the stub of a large cigar.

Classy thugs, I remember thinking as I left.

Feeling under the thumb of this latest dilemma, I hopped in my truck and drove around, trying to come up with a painless solution. I could call the police, but then they would arrest Adrian for possession and she would lose her job. Plus, this would put the police in the parking lot for hours; all the other tenants would see the commotion. And hell of hells, something like that might invalidate my leases. If anyone wanted to leave, for whatever reason, the fact that a drug bust had occurred would give them a good argument out of the lease. Then, a court case would probably take six months to a year for Adrian, and in the end, she still might not have gotten convicted. If no conviction was leveled, we'd have had no justification for evicting her. We would wind up with a pissed off non-convicted tenant.

What a mess.

Having some time to calm myself a little, I came to the firm belief that it was Adrian's boyfriend who was to blame. I figured he had probably followed her from Dadson's Mill and was just using her for her nice new place. His nasty little habits would probably devastate her career. She would end up without a job and back in Dadson's Mills, no future in sight.

But then, what about the children she was teaching? Didn't the school need this information to protect the children? And what about me? I was a state police officer – didn't I have the responsibility to arrest her?

After driving in a circle for an hour, I decided that I had but a tiny bit of evidence; not nearly enough to go on.

After all, I had seen only remnants of smoking and firmly believed that these remnants were not hers. She was working as a teacher, and I knew the school system tested teachers for drugs.

So I came up with a solution. I went home and typed a form letter addressed to me from her. "Dear Mr. Reid," it read, "As per our phone call, due to a family emergency, I must terminate my residence at your apartment immediately. I understand that I will receive a full refund of my deposit if I vacate the property today." I made sure to leave a space for her signature and the date.

Meanwhile, I called Jackie and told her about the problem. My wife let me know how I could get to the school where Adrian worked. I drove the forty miles and went straight to the office.

"I've got an emergency," I told the secretary. "I've got to speak to one of your teachers."

When Adrian arrived, I asked her if we could speak in private. She agreed. Once in the clear, I informed her that

I had performed a maintenance service in her apartment and discovered marijuana cigarettes in the living room. I could tell from her face that she was terrified.

"I figure its people from Dadson's Mills bringing you down," I told her. "And I understand how hard it can be to escape the past. But I just can't tolerate it."

She looked ready to cry.

"I'm here to offer you a choice, Adrian," I continued, handing her the letter. "Either you can sign this and come with me. I'll move you out today, if you do. Or I'm going to call the police and have them arrest you when you get home this afternoon."

She read the letter, eagerly agreeing to sign it and get out. She apologized and thanked me profusely for the second chance. I could tell that the principal and secretary really liked her, because they insisted that she leave immediately to handle the "emergency."

The Dealers (Revisited) Lesson #2: Even the worst offenders deserve a second chance. At least if they're sweet little school teachers trying to break away from the projects...

Adrian had enough money for a U-Haul, but not enough to rent a storage unit. So I gave her $40 cash for a storage unit as an advance from her security deposit.

When the whole scene had ended, I called the detective and told him that I had moved the problem tenant out. He thanked me.

From then on, I noticed that I was receiving better service from the police department. Background checks and reference calls became a lot easier. I guess the police figured that I'd helped them eliminate a nest for drug dealers, so they would scratch my back in return.

Throughout this ordeal, the shame of the Marvin crackhouse stuck to the back of my mind. I had botched handling that situation, and as a result, had put the whole neighborhood in danger.

So here's the final Dealer's lesson: Rapid response is a much better way to deal with drug dealers than waiting for them to show up at the unit. You have to jump when something like this comes up because you have other families depending on you for safe and peaceful housing.

The Perverts

You just never know, reader. Even the nicest folks – the ones you're *certain* have a good head on their shoulders – turn out to be creeps. Speaking of creeps let me tell you about maybe our creepiest tenant: Tony (or "Quido," as everyone called him).

Quido was a potbellied guy who had just returned to the country from the Philippines. He had secured a job at a place called Steel Containers, working as the nightshift manager.

Quido enters the scene when I was tooling around the old pool building one day and got the feeling that someone was standing beside me. I turned to see who it was, jumping back because Quido startled the crap out of me. He was standing right behind me, you see. He had just been watching what I was doing and breathing hard through his mouth.

"You scared the shit out of me," I said, noticing that Quido was shirtless, wearing nothing but loose gym shorts and flip-flops.

He laughed, and then tried to start making small talk.

I wasn't having any of it. Instead, I tried easing my way out of the pool building. I mean, it looked like he might have something going on in his shorts, forgodsakes.

Once I got my wits about me, I said, "Look, Tony...I'm sure everyone walks around half naked like this in the Philippines, but this is Alabama, and you're in an apartment complex. You can't be walking around here with your junk hanging out."

"Oh," he said pensively.

I continued telling him that this was a family complex with children and single mothers. "They might get the idea that you're creepy," I said.

"Oh, Pat," he replied, "I didn't even think about that."

I almost laughed as I took in his greasy, jet-black hair and potbelly. He had absolutely no muscle tone. I only mention this because his attitude didn't match his physique. It was clear he thought he was God's gift to women. But reader, he was gross. Just to give you an idea: Jackie had one tenant ask her about him. Believe me; this tenant didn't want a date. Rather, she told Jackie that she thought he looked strange and might be a bit of a perv. I dismissed it all, thinking maybe it was all just a little too cynical or overly suspicious.

A couple of months passed. Quido called in to ask if we would be willing to rent a vacant apartment to his ex-wife, Cherry, and their daughter. Apparently Cherry wasn't working because she couldn't walk. She got a check from the military each month. Jackie and I were all for it, figuring that having Anthony's ex around would prevent him from strutting around the property in his skivvies. Besides, Cherry was quiet and shy and she always paid her rent on time.

As an aside, every now and then, Jackie and I would go to the local bar, where we would dance to a jukebox. Cherry and Quido would show up and immediately clear the dance floor with their Saturday night moves. Jackie made the comment that Cherry got around pretty well for someone who couldn't walk.

Anyway, after a few months, Quido moved in with Cherry. After the move-in, they immediately installed a hot tub on the back deck, which was made of concrete. Cherry "needed" this hot tub because it was a part of her "physical therapy," I'm told. Within a few days, they had strung a blue tarp from the second story to the top of the fence across the yard. I guess it was for privacy. Normally, I'd have demanded that they take down such an eyesore, but none of my tenants complained about it. I guess they were like us, thinking it far better not to have to look at those two in a hot tub. The benefits outweighed the drawbacks, I suppose.

One day, Quido called Jackie, asking for the number to the women's shelter where my wife worked. He also wanted to know the address. Jackie gave him the number, but told him that the location was confidential. Turns out, he wanted the number so he could call a coworker of Jackie's. It wasn't long after this that the coworker mentioned to Jackie that she thought Quido and Cherry were swingers. They had met her at a local bar one evening and wanted her to go home with them and get into the hot tub.

Weird people, man. Fortunately, they got out.

Unfortunately, reader, they'd only be the first on a long list of weirdos.

A really sweet guy who worked for a Survey company lived in one of our apartments with his very shy wife and two cute children. He was soft-spoken, this guy – and we'll call him Willy.

One afternoon, I got a call from Willy's wife explaining that a tall, skinny man was showing up at the apartment complex and scaring the life out of her. So I met with her. It was clear that she, too, had a severe handicap, but she described the guy who was showing up at the apartment complex well enough. And I knew exactly who she was talking about because he was a streetwalker and I had seen him around before. I told her that I would take care of it.

As an aside, some time later when I was there to fix her sink, she talked about her children. Jackie and I had noticed that the children rode the "short bus" to school, which meant that they were mentally challenged. Willy's wife was so proud of them, explaining that she hoped that they wouldn't be autistic. She explained that they had both been born handicapped.

I wish you could have met her husband, reader. Willy was a sweet man and a good father and provider. Every Wednesday night, he would have his little family dressed for dinner in their Sunday best. He was as proud and happy as anyone I ever met.

Anyway, aside over. A few days later, I found out the streetwalker was back and had bummed $5 off them, promising the family that he would never come back if they paid him what he wanted. Surprise, surprise, he didn't keep his promise. He would always time his visits for when Willy was at work. I guess he knew the woman of the house was scared, so he would harass her like a predator.

You've probably seen guys like him. Jackie called him "Happy Britches." He was about 5'11" with gray hair and a smile with just a handful of teeth that showed. He was notorious around the neighborhood about asking people for money at the gas stations and fast food restaurants. If you gave him a dollar, he would look in your wallet and ask for the five. He was always trying to get close to you, a sinister look in his eye.

Whenever he did it to me, I would yell at him to get back. Then, he would skulk away all dejected and I would feel bad about it. Even though I'd just given him money!

He looked like a crack abuser, but he was in fact a predator. The perverted kind. Since he was always invading the complex, I went to the municipal court and filed a trespass warning on him. He disappeared for a while after getting served the warning.

But all good things must come to an end. One night, a tenant called because her vehicle window had been smashed and the radio had been stolen. I stood in the dark with Officer Jenkins, discussing the incident. While we were talking, Happy Britches came juking up and butted his head in.

"Officer," I said, pointing at HB, "this guy is trespassing. I've got a warning issued against him already."

The officer reminded HB about the warning by getting up in his face and telling him not to come back on the property.

Again, Happy Britches left and I didn't see him for some time. He finally quit bothering the quiet family and the complex had peace once again.

Round about this same time, Hasselville experienced an influx of Vietnamese families. Many of them opened up nail and beauty shops in the area. One group rented two apartments from us. They were the nicest tenants you could ever meet, reader. One family had a little girl named Mercedes who loved to play outside. She was about five years old.

One day, I saw the infamous Louis playing with a kid from the neighborhood. Louis was laughing hysterically. As I passed by, I asked what was so funny.

He pointed at the other kid. "He told Mercedes to pull her pants down."

I laid into him about how wrong all that was. Then, I told the offending kid that he wasn't welcome around the property anymore. And finally, I called Shaquikwa and told her to get her shit together regarding Louis. He couldn't just run around anymore, I explained.

The incident with little Mercedes terrified Jackie and me. The parents of these boys obviously didn't care and weren't about to waste their time supervising them. Jackie called Mercedes' parents to let them know what had happened and to explain that Louis was mentally challenged and going through puberty. They got the hint: Mercedes shouldn't be running around outside without supervision.

Their daughter had already told them about pulling down her pants. Apparently, she had thought it was funny, too. But her parents straightened her out and thanked us for letting them about know the situation.

Fortunately, a potential solution to the problem presented itself a couple of days later. See, one of Shaquikwa loser boyfriends had caused some trouble – creating a bad domestic abuse scene on the property – and it proved a good opportunity to make Shaquikwa and her pervert son pack their things.

When I told Shaquikwa she would have to move out, she cried and said she didn't have anywhere to go. Naturally,

I felt bad. I had more apartments across the highway, two blocks down. So I thought maybe they could live there and leave these problems behind.

The school was within walking distance for Louis, too, so that was nice. Plus, the building was a four-plex and we didn't have any other teenagers living there. Shaquikwa agreed to make the move.

Perverts Lesson #1: Two blocks just ain't far enough.

Shaquikwa and son weren't in their new place a good month before Jackie received a call from a woman who lived in the house behind the four-plex.

"I just saw two teenage kids having sex on the back patio," the hysterical woman belted. "You gotta do something about this."

So we sighed and got in the truck to go talk to Shaquikwa.

Shaquikwa opened the door and immediately told us she didn't know what was going on. We were furious because we knew that Louis was headed for trouble and Shaquikwa didn't seem to give a damn. I got the strong impression that she was proud of Louis. After all, he was only fifteen years old.

Since mom was no help, I walked around back to investigate. There, I found a used condom on the patio. More than one. They'd been doing this for weeks, it seemed. And suddenly, something occurred to me: these weren't the first used condoms I'd found on my property. In fact, I'd been finding them all over the front lawn of the complex Shaquikwa and son had just vacated. Louis had been screwing for *months*.

"That's it, Shaquikwa," I said when I went back inside. "We're through with you. You've got to get out. Start looking for a new place. You move out ASAP."

I washed my hands of it, figuring I could drop by the next day and find Shaquikwa moving her things into a van. Instead, when I knocked on the door, I saw that she had moved her brother in with her. Two other guys were sleeping on the floor, too.

"Who are these people?" I asked.

"My boyfriend's friends," she said matter-of-factly.

These guys had "drug dealer" and "thug" written all over them. Shaquikwa, it seemed, was making no effort to find a new place.

One day, I stopped by because the thugs from the living room were sitting on the porch, drinking beer. I walked right past them and knocked on the door. When Shaquikwa finally opened it, I told her that I wasn't going to have grown men sitting on the porch, drinking beer all day.

"They ain't drinking beer," she said.

So I picked one of the cups up off the porch and smelled its contents. "It ain't lemonade," I said.

At that moment, Louis walked around from the back of the apartment, drinking beer from a glass. "Are you drinking beer?" I asked him.

"He just getting that beer for me," one of the thugs said.

But then, Louis stumbled, clearly drunk.

That was it for me. I lost it. "Shaquikwa," I hollered, "I'm calling Jackie. And she's going to type you a notice to get out within ten days. I've tried everything I can think of to work with you. But now we're through."

Both of the thugs slurred something threatening.

I just stared at them. "You look like you have warrants," I said. I picked up my cell phone and called the police, asking them to send a unit over.

Not another word from the thugs. They just went quietly inside and closed the door.

"If you're here after the tenth day," I said to Shaquikwa, "then, I'll file for eviction. That'll make it near impossible for you to even get into government housing."

Shaquikwa stormed inside. I knew exactly what she was doing: calling Jackie, the good cop in our little good cop, bad cop arrangement.

Jackie later told me that she gave Shaquikwa the telephone numbers to all the government housing complexes in the area. So at least this ridiculous tenant was making the effort. Still, I could hardly stand the next ten days. Whenever I drove by the apartment, those thugs would be out drinking on the porch. Non-stop.

Shaquikwa finally got an apartment, but had to wait two weeks while it was being renovated. When she finally drove off, I exhaled like a balloon.

I put a note on the neighbor's door, letting them know that Shaquikwa and crew were gone. I'm sure they were relieved. Jackie then called the woman who lived in the house behind the four-plex and gave her the good news. She was delighted.

I wish I could say that that was the end of our pervert issues. Mentally challenged teenage boys are one thing, but sometimes, the sexually deviant come from the places you least expect.

You remember Arnold, our first resident manager (the one we had to fire). Well, one of the things that creeped Jackie out about him was that he was always babysitting. More accurately, he was always babysitting for young boys. For whatever reason, his adult friends always let their boys stay with him. He was a youth minister in a local church, I gathered.

One weekend, Jackie and I planned a trip to the beach with a co-worker and his wife. They knew Arnold and thought he was a great guy and a great fisherman. I figured it would be great to fish from the jet skis we had recently purchased. Arnold had a jet ski, took, so we asked him if he would like to go. Now, our boys were about ten years old at the time, so they couldn't ride the jet skis without a partner. Obviously, Arnold would always volunteer to take them.

Well, Arnold headed straight out for the gulf. When he'd gotten far enough away from shore, he shut down the jet ski and was just drifting over the waves talking to our son. Jackie watched him like a hawk and waved them to come back into shore. When he got back in to shore, she put a stop to that shit.

That night, while we were cooking out on the patio, the boys went to the swimming pool. We were sitting around and talking when we noticed that Arnold was in the pool with the boys.

"Shouldn't he be up here with the adults?" I asked my wife. *Bing!* I finally got it.

So I went over to the pool and told the boys to come up and eat. I didn't let them go back. Arnold stayed in the pool all by himself. It was a bit like watching an alligator cruise around.

That night, we were getting ready to go to bed. My coworker and his wife were sleeping in the twin beds in the guest room. The boys brought their sleeping bags and Jackie helped them set up camp in our bedroom. The couch in the living room made out into a bed, so Arnold slept there. When I say "slept," I mean it only relatively. At one point during the night, I got up to check on him and he was on his laptop. At another point, I got up to take a piss and he was curled up in the fetal position on the floor. And then finally, I needed a glass of water. He was back on the laptop again.

That was about it for us. We knew we couldn't have a pervert traipsing around the apartment complex. So we'd fired him and now it was time to kick him out.

Later, I went to a website and looked up the signs of a pedophile. Arnold had all the signs. He even stocked candy in his refrigerator at the apartment. If he wasn't a creep...well, he sure fooled us!

Arnold had a rough past with a loser mother and abusive boyfriends, so I felt bad about getting rid of him. Plus, we never had a complaint about Arnold while he lived at the complex. We just felt he was a little too into kids for our taste. It was certainly possible that Arnold just liked kids and was perfectly harmless. But I figured it was better to err on the side of safety. We never dealt with him again.

Problems with Pets

Now the following story isn't about an apartment complex tenant, but it's just too good not to include here. Let me tell you, reader, it doesn't matter what level of tenant-income you're renting to, here; you're going to find yourself dealing with pets of all sorts.

Anyway, on to the story. You'll recall Anna, the seductress who answered her door in an open nightgown. Well, after she finally left (following that whole fiasco), I was fixing up her vacated unit when Christy, a woman who rented from me in an apartment down the street, approached me with her sister, Winnie. Winnie needed an apartment, see. Well, needless to say, she loved the unit. It was clear that the biggest perk would be that she would be living down the street from her sister. As an aside, I'm not sure what was wrong with Winnie, but whenever she opened her mouth to talk, it was like she was hollering. It was kind of unnerving.

Jackie met with Winnie and the two of them completed the application. As we discovered, Winnie received some government checks every month – and she also had a boyfriend/fiancé who was supposed to help with the bills. Right. Winnie was constantly late with her $250 rent payment. It was always a hassle. Jackie would call Winnie's mother to inform. Winnie's mother would in turn pay the rent. I guess she just didn't want her daughter moving in with her.

For months, Winnie's mom paid the rent. I can't tell you how many times we were at the end of our rope and would start to evict Winnie – mostly because of other disorderly actions. Most of them stemmed from the goddamned dog. See, Winnie had a son and a daughter. Her son – a kid who eventually became an angry young man – got a puppy one day. They kept the dog for years. And it was insane. Part of the problem? They kept it inside in a pen that was far too small. Whenever someone went to their apartment, the dog would go all "white eyed" and bark the whole time. That dog really creeped me out.

I told Winnie to do something about the dog – maybe get a bigger crate or give it to someone with some sense. It was sick seeing that insane dog snarling in that tiny cage. I mean, he didn't have any room to move. His fur would stick though the wire. It was horrible. But I could tell that the family and Winnie enjoyed the reactions they got from people about this dog. I guess it was some kind of loony power trip derived from people being leery of the animal.

Problems with Pets Lesson #1: Your tenants will use their vicious dogs to scare you. Seriously. Maybe take a defense against dogs class. *Seriously*.

After the chronic complainer moved out, we got a call from a guy who needed an apartment. He worked at an auto beauty shop business as the head painter. Here's the scenario: The owner had highly recommended this guy, he definitely made enough money to pay the rent, and it seemed reasonable to give him a lease. So we gave him a lease.

This painter, we'll call him Jerry, moved in and was never a problem...until he moved his girlfriend in with him. She was cute, but strange. She liked to lie in the sun at the pool during the day. Was that strange? Of course not. But it's important later, so I thought I'd throw it in here.

Now, we had previously rented an apartment close to Jerry and his girlfriend. The tenants? Two single firemen. It wasn't a week after Jerry's girl moved in that we saw her talking to one of the firemen near the pool and sneaking around the complex with him. Jerry was always working and making a lot of cash, but his girlfriend was evidently enjoying the company of the good looking fireman.

Naturally, the boyfriend got mad – mad enough to take a job with another auto shop and move the two of them out of the apartment without completing the lease. I know what you're thinking. *This is an adultery story, right? Or a story about tenants who skipped out on their responsibilities... What's this got to do with pets?*

Good questions, reader. Let me tell you, I was as surprised as anyone to find out that this was a pet story.

How did I discover it? I went into Jerry's apartment after they had skipped town. The weird thing was what I noticed in the front bedroom upstairs: a tree limb strung up to the ceiling and tied to a rope that traveled all the way into the closet. The bulb in the bedroom's overhead light was out, so the only light I had to deal with was that coming in from behind the closed curtains – just enough light to grant me a sense of the shadow of things.

Nearly blind, I followed the rope to the closet. Just as I stepped up to it, a rat sprang out and jumped onto my face. I screamed and threw it down, hauling ass outside. Picture me standing there, quivering like a schoolgirl, wiping invisible critters off my face and neck. I was freaked.

Anyway, after I calmed down, I grabbed the largest stick I could find and went back inside. I could just see Jackie showing this apartment and the rat jumping on her.

Slowly, I crept up the stairs, surveying the floors and walls as I walked. I looked at the bedroom door, which had somehow closed when I'd fled. My heart racing, I opened the door. *You used to chase night hunters with guns, Patrick,* I thought. *Come on, man.*

I froze as I saw a small, dark animal on the floor, grooming itself in the very dim light. *What the fuck is that?* I asked myself. It looked like a bat or something.

Quietly, I closed the door and went to search for a flashlight. Having found one, I returned with light blazing. When I shined it into the room, the thing from the closet took off. I heard its little feet thumping on the floor. Then, it jumped or flew for the closet – I'm not really sure – I just kept hearing these weird thumping noises. When it was in, I slammed the closet door shut. Then, I immediately cut down the rope and tree limb. As it hit the floor, I noticed that the carpet was covered with droppings that I couldn't identify. Turns everywhere.

One thing seemed clear: the painter and his girlfriend had been using this whole bedroom as a pen for something.

So I called a friend who fancied himself a bit of an expert on animals. "I think there's some kind of flying squirrel or something in the closet," I said. "What should I do?"

"What do you mean?" my friend asked.

"Well, I don't want to shoot it or club it to death. I'd rather catch it, if I can."

I know what you're thinking, reader: Oh, he doesn't want to hurt the little animal; how sweet. But really, I could've given a shit about the bat/rat/thing. I just didn't want to shoot a hole in the sheetrock or cause the animal to bleed all over the place and ruin up my carpet.

Anyway, my friend had something for me. "Just get plenty of light on it and pick it up," he said.

So I did that. Sure enough, the little squirrel rolled up and hid his face.

"That worked," I said.

"Yep," my friend said. "Back before television—" (this friend had silver hair and was much older than me, see) "—all the kids where I grew up would try catching the flying squirrels as pets. After we'd catch one, we'd put them in a sock."

"A sock?" I said incredulously. "What the hell for?"

"You catch him in the sock, then spin him around in a circle over your head. Like that big machine astronauts use for training."

"That's crazy."

"No, no," he said. "It makes them really dizzy, which for some reason tames them right away."

I chuckled, thinking about swinging this little guy around my head.

"They're great little pets," he added.

"Yeah, until they attack your face," I said. I hung up with my friend and carried the cute little fellow out into the woods behind my house. It felt good to do the right thing in this case; felt good not to hurt him.

Not three months later, I began hearing the unmistakable sounds of scurrying in the ceiling of my house. Suddenly, I had a flying squirrel colony in my attic and they were chewing up the wiring. How we got them out of our house and attic is a whole book in itself, so I won't get into that here. Suffice to say, my boys had a great time and were clearly fascinated by it. Just goes to show you; no good deed ever goes unpunished.

So with a complex now free of flying squirrels and cat-men, Jackie and I had a few peaceful days pass. A few. Then, we had one of our tenants turn up with a snow white cat with a bobbed tail. I furrowed my brow at the tenant, but he told me that his daughter really wanted this cat. Aw. But then I looked at his carpet and saw that the cat had already shredded the seams between the rooms.

"Look," I said. "You can keep the cat, but you can't let it be a yard cat. You've got to keep it in here."

The man nodded.

"And keep an eye on the carpets," I said.

The guy tried for a few months, but I guess after a while he just grew tired of the litter box. A couple of times, I saw his daughter walking the cat on a leash. I'd never seen that sort of thing before, but obviously it didn't work out for long. Soon, the cat was wandering around the complex.

Pets Lesson #2: Cats. They wander. It's a fact of life. If you're going to allow your tenants to keep the little bastards, expect to see them all over the place.

I wanted to get angry, but the problem was that this was the prettiest and sweetest cat you've ever seen and most of the tenants adored it. Jackie'd even given it a name: Snowball. And she loved it, too.

Snowball would lie in the middle of the parking lot. Sometimes, she'd get up behind cars and wouldn't move no matter what. Everyone just did what they could to drive around him.

One day, I was talking to the owner when I told him that Snowball was going to get killed laying around like that.

"Yeah," he said. "I just found out that that cat's deaf as a doorknob. That's why he doesn't get out of the way when you yell at him." He laughed.

I didn't say anything else because I figured that between a deaf cat and about a dozen cars, the problem would take care of itself. But damnit, reader, that cat had a hundred lives. It lived there for years. Hell, it still may live there as I'm writing this.

The Last Word on Complex Tenants

Pun intended. If you haven't noticed already, renters at apartment complexes tend to be, well, complex. You've read about the perverts and the weirdos and the pet owners. You've been privy to the thugs and the dealers and the sexually promiscuous. But allow me to close out this chapter with a story that offers a little bit of everything. And let's kick it off with our final lesson of the chapter:

Final Lesson of the Chapter: In this business, a vacancy causes a lot of anxiety, so it's tempting to take someone at face value when they show up with a handful of cash. Don't succumb to the temptation.

I had just finished renovating a unit when a guy – we'll call him Mr. McLeery – drove up in a big white truck with two little kids. He got out, big as the world, and told me that he was looking for an apartment.

"I lay carpet for a living," he claimed.

Shortly, his wife drove up with his mother. The wife had black and purple hair. Her short, stubby fingers were painted with black fingernail polish. Sure, you city folks see this all the time, but trust me, I'd never seen anyone in that kind of getup in our small town.

So McLeery's mother and wife got out of the car and introduced themselves. They looked exhausted – and probably were because they'd driven to Hasselville from Ohio. From the point his mother set foot on the grass, she did most of the talking. She proved willing to sign the lease for her adult son and his family. Should have been a red flag, reader. Should have been a red flag.

But they all seemed so nice, so we accepted the cash and put the whole gang down on the lease.

As time went by, McLeery seemed to exhibit behaviors associated with the bi-polar disorder – but as it would turn out, he was just a nutty, crooked mama's boy. I should have known he was going to be trouble the day he backed out of the driveway and his big truck snagged the cable wire, yanking it loose. Didn't seem to bother him, this damage he'd accidentally caused.

McLeery was always away on business, so his mother would often pick up the kids and take them to her grand home in the country. Meanwhile, his "Goth" wife would hang around the apartment, spying out their front window. Occasionally, I would catch a glimpse of her black fingernails as she hid behind the drapes.

One day, I was at the unit, working in the yard. My landscaper had hired a thin, frail guy to work the weed-eater, which was loud as hell. Despite the noise, the "Goth" girl was able to follow the guy around, talking to him all afternoon. It looked to me like she was trying to get him to come into her apartment. I guess she could have been talking to him about the weather. Or given our luck, maybe she was fishing for a crack connection.

I don't know what she said to him, but later on, when I was coming around by my storage building, the weed-eater guy stepped out and addressed me by my first name. I didn't know this guy from Adam, but he was talking to me like we were long lost buddies.

"What are you doing in my tool building?" I asked him.

"Just taking a break," he said.

"This is a private building," I said. "You shouldn't be in here."

"Okay," he said, grinning. Whatever Ms. Goth did to him in that building, she sure empowered the little shit.

A couple weeks later, I went into the happy home of McLeery and Goth with the intention of changing the air filter. To my anger and dismay, I found that my tenants had changed the locks on me. So I knocked on the door. The second I knocked, I heard a dog barking. When I looked through the window, I could see that it was a chow/pit mix.

I waited for a long while, but nobody answered the door. So I called McLeery at work and told him he'd have to get rid of the dog.

"But my kids love that dog," he said. "I'd hate to have to get rid of it."

"I'm sorry," I said, "but the only thing that breed of a dog is likely to do is bite your kids or another tenant."

Silence.

"Why don't you take him to your mom's house? She lives in the country, right?"

"Alright, alright," he said. "I'll get rid of the dog."

"Promise me," I said.

"I promise."

McLeery held his promise for about a week. The priceless part was that he must have thought he was fooling me. I would later learn that McLeery had actually given the dog away, but that the owners had made him take it back after it bit one of their kids. When I discovered the situation, he assured me that he would get rid of the dog.

"How can I trust you this time?" I asked.

"My mother-in-law just leased a portion of the Rosenstein warehouse. You know the place?"

I nodded. A warehouse on the outskirts of town being converted into retail locations.

"She's going to put a pet store in there and I'm going to help her run it."

"Do you know anything about the pet business?" I asked.

"I know all about the pet business. I've had dogs and snakes my whole life. And we're getting a deal on the location because we're taking care of the renovations on our portion of the warehouse."

I shook my head because I knew Rosenstein. He probably figured he would get this idiot McLeery to fix up the warehouse for free, figuring he had nothing to lose in a desolate area of town where no one else would ever consider renting commercial property. I'm sure Rosenstein had put this poor bastard on a lease just to get him working.

As if adultery and dogs and pet stores weren't enough, one night, we got a call from the fire department. They'd had to visit one of our complexes. Guess which one. Luckily, there was no considerable damage. When we arrived, it was no surprise to learn that the fire had originated in McLeery's kitchen. His wife was cooking the kids a frozen pizza and had forgotten about it while they were swimming in the pool.

At that point, McLeery was unemployed and way behind on his rent, so I told him they had to go. They disappeared one night and that was the last we ever saw of them. If only I could say that they left the apartment without incident.

But I can't. See, when Jackie and I went into the apartment, we discovered a horrible mess. Everything was broken. Every piece of drywall, every window, every cabinet, the stove, the refrigerator, the dishwasher. The dishwasher! Who breaks a dishwasher? McLeery had stuck a piece of metal into the tub of the appliance, one end of it touching the large heating element that lines the bottom of most dishwashers. The heating element had heated the piece of metal, which in turn melted through the racks and sides of the dishwasher. I was stunned. I mean, I never would've imagined a dishwasher being destroyed like that.

Let's talk about the carpet. McLeery had removed the living room carpet and appeared to have used the room as a kennel. I guess this made it easier for Goth or the kids to scoop the dog shit off the concrete slab.

The trail of damage went right up the stairs, as well. Crayon drawings all over the walls. Holes punched in the sheetrock. Missing door knobs. A missing showerhead. Even the mirror in the medicine cabinet was cracked.

While I say that McLeery and family destroyed the apartment, I don't think they intentionally beat the crap out of it. I think they'd just managed to break all of this stuff along the way. Some of the damage appeared as if they had attempted and failed to fix things.

Jackie and I photographed the unit and prepared for our case in court.

Jackie called Rosenstein, the landlord for McLeery's halfassed pet shop deal, and told him that she was trying to track down our wayward tenant. Rosenstein was more than happy to help her, since he was getting stiffed at the same time.

"I got McLeery's mother to sign the lease," my wife said.

Rosenstein seemed pleased because he knew we could collect from the mother, if not from the son. See, McLeery had tried to get out of his lease with Mr. Rosenstein for the so-called pet store, but he wouldn't let him. Shortly thereafter, the building caught fire. The part of the building that had been destroyed had been chalked up to old wiring. But then, how convenient for the McLeerys...

After Jackie found the address for McLeery's mother, we got in the truck and headed out to the rural location. When we knocked on the door, she opened it almost immediately, her husband standing behind her. Jackie presented her with an itemized bill, which only amounted to $1,900 because I had made an effort to depreciate the damaged materials. She took the bill and thanked us.

As she closed the door, I heard her husband yell at her. "You shouldn't have signed that damn lease," he said.

The husband was a big wig at an industrial plant in Hasselville, so I guess he couldn't take being told what to do for too long. Just as we got out to the car, he came outside and stopped us.

"We don't have to pay for this," he said angrily. "Now get off my property."

I calmly looked out the window of my car and up at his house. "You've got a nice place," I said. "You might regret not paying that debt if the courts decide to sell your wife's half to cover the damages."

He stood in the grass, looking so angry he could spit.

"Have a great day," Jackie said. And then we left. I remember how red the fat-faced man was as we drove off.

Jackie went to the courthouse the next day and filed the paperwork to sue for damages. I guess it must have shaken them up, because we soon got a call from the big shot attorney they hired. He said he wanted a copy of the lease. Jackie took the damaged pictures, but not the lease to the attorney's office because I'd looked at the lease and noticed that the bitch had signed the wrong side. I worried that we might not be covered. So I called the attorney after my wife had been there with the pictures.

"She has a lease," I told him. "She knows what damage was done and she knows that she agreed to be legally responsible for her son."

I knew we might not have a case, but we wanted our day in court to show the pictures to the judge. McLeery's mother, I figure, didn't feel the same way. Plus, I'm sure the big shot attorney didn't want to waste his afternoon battling this nonsense in front of a judge. But he did something I wasn't expecting.

"I'll drag this case out for years," he threatened.

That one threw me for a loop. But I wasn't just going to sit back and take it. So I called the judge and told him that the defendant's attorney called and threatened to continue the case for years.

"I might grant one extension," the judge said. "But definitely no more than a month's delay.

This was a surprising response, since I knew that that judge didn't particularly care for me. I guess he just despised that particular big shot attorney.

The attorney tried to get an extension and failed. He called the next week, offering a $500 settlement. We rejected it, saying we would consider $1,500. It wasn't long before he called back and said he had our check.

So that's it, reader. Sometimes, when your tenants knock you for a loop, you just have to knock back. There might be times when you get so overwhelmed with the crap you have to deal with on an almost daily basis that you don't know how you'll get by. The most important lesson of this entire book, then, is to never give up. Never give up, reader. If you get to the point where you have nearly daily tenant-related headaches, then you're probably also to the point where you've got loads of money rolling in – or at least you're on the cusp of reaching that critical mass. Money, as they say, solves a whole lot of problems.

Unfortunately, until you get to the point where Jackie and I are today, those problems might be many.

Chapter Twelve

The title of this chapter might seem a little odd. What we're going to do here is leave you with a slew of stories that just didn't fit conceptually into the earlier chapters – stories that were just too juicy to exclude. The chapter title refers to a particularly troubling apartment complex that we purchased, one with only twelve of twenty-four units occupied. We dealt with so many headaches and heartaches with this place, it's a wonder we still own it.

Again, we don't mean to deter you from the big money that can be made in this business. You just have to read to believe some of the shit that goes on in these places.

One of the more disturbing situations to crop up at twelve of twenty-four was at an apartment rented to two couples. Why was it disturbing? The males in each couple were skinheads. Funny, though...the skinheads on their own weren't an issue. It wasn't until we later rented a unit a couple of doors down to two Coast Guard employees

357

that all hell began to break loose. As soon as the Coast Guard moved in, problems started.

One morning at about 3am, I got a call that one of the skinheads was standing on the brick wall surrounding the complex, peeing into the night. Incidentally, this night happened to be the night the Coast Guard contingent had invited all their buddies over for an apartment warming party.

So, sleepy as all hell, I drove over to stop the party. I looked up the skinheads first. Obviously, as they said, the trouble wasn't their fault.

"What?" I said incredulously. "Did the Coast Guards *force* you to get naked and pee off the wall?"

The other skinhead – the one who wasn't purported to have done the pissing – looked at me calmly and said, "No, we're talking about the police coming out."

"What?" I repeated, stunned.

"Yep. The police had to come, you see. We were partying with the Coast Guard guys and they got naked. And that blonde little guy touched my penis and said he was gay."

One of the Coast Guards' friends was a tiny bleached blonde guy, I would later discover. Apparently, when the skinhead told his lover what had happened, the lover hit the little blonde guy and they left. Then the skinheads realized one of their wallets was missing, so they went back and kicked the door in, searching for it. That's when the police were called.

"I don't need to hear any more," I said, waving my hand in the air in frustration. "I want to make it clear that no amount of money or effort will allow you to stay."

They nodded stupidly.

"I'm now going to make every effort and use every tool available to ensure that you are removed from this property."

The talkative skinhead tried to interrupt me with an excuse, but I put my hand up and said, "We're finished doing business. Do you understand?"

They shook their heads yes, their mouths hanging open.

Jackie and I went back the next day to find that they were ready to leave. My wife wrote them a check for the deposit and we never heard from them again.

Around that time, we had to find a balance in bringing this property back from the brink. We were experiencing a whole lot of mortgage debt and initially, the property was only half rented. It was clear that we had to fill it up without spending a fortune on renovations. But all the units needed appliances, fixtures, and carpeting. To make matters worse, the walls had cheap, thin paneling, making them difficult to dress up nicely. I tried painting, but that didn't work. Then, in one unit, I tried to put up sheetrock. The problem with sheetrock is that at least three coats of paint are required, and that wasn't going to hold up in this place. So I finally hired a drywall guy to do two units. He did his part in a couple of days, but it took me a couple of weeks to finish all the details and trim.

One day, while I was checking on the drywall guys, I saw an old 1970 Toyota pull up. I watched as a couple in their late thirties or early forties got out of the car. The guy had to pop the hood and disconnect the battery in order to turn off the old thing. They walked right up and told me that they were looking for an apartment.

"Hammerick," he said. "My name's Hammerick."

So I learned that Mr. Hammerick had a job at Winston Company, a plumbing outfit. He had returned to Hasselville to work on a big job, from what I gathered.

Even before we finished our conversation, I had already made a decision not to do business with them. But for whatever reason, I smiled and told them that unit 1742 was ready to be rented.

"Go on up and check it out while I finish up here," I said. I don't know why.

I was still loading the tools in my truck when they came back out from "inspecting the apartment." The girl, I kid you not, was limping. She had "tripped on the stairs."

"Hey man," the guy said. "Your handrail came loose and she hurt herself."

The display was pathetic. I'd been set up. And I felt like an idiot.

"Oh," I said. "I'm so sorry." I immediately went to check out the handrail. Well I'll be damned if someone hadn't unscrewed that rail.

I stood in the apartment and looked at the couple, who'd limped up behind me. Since this guy claimed to work at Winston, I figured that he shouldn't have any trouble paying the rent if we had anything available. So I came up with a plan.

"I've got another unit I can show you," I said. "Newly installed drywall."

They liked it and moved in that evening. Again, I don't know what I was thinking. Stupid, stupid move, Patrick. But, reader, they paid the deposit and first month's rent in cash, so that seemed cool.

I guess I was just scared they might file a lawsuit if I didn't let them rent. At the time, I had a contract to manage the apartments and pay the owner a mortgage amount, so I wasn't about to get tied up in legal trouble. Besides, the owner was paying for insurance and I wasn't sure I would be covered if the girl sued me.

For her "injury," the girl started going to the doctor to get painkillers. They even told her she needed physical therapy. I'd been to physical therapy before. The bill was $450. I was terrified I'd get stuck with a similar bill this time around.

But I'm a proactive guy, reader. I knew the chief of security at Southern States, an industrial company. He had special training dealing with fraud cases. I spoke with him about my situation because I knew he had access to time-lapsed video cameras and recorders. He loaned me the equipment and installed the cameras upstairs in the window of the adjacent apartment. I had a clear few of the front yard and parking lot. For weeks I recorded evidence of this woman walking sometimes running to and from her car.

It was actually quite simple. In the morning, she would walk to the car and take the kids to school. Around noon, she would go to lunch. And then around 3pm, she would go back to school to pick up the kids. I recorded hours and hours of her on video, all of them featuring her walking without a limp. But then, whenever she would go to the doctor, she would come out with a crutch and a leg brace.

She really put on a show. But after she got her meds, she would drop off the crutch and brace in the front seat of the Toyota, which no longer ran.

Every morning, just for good measure, I would buy a newspaper and put it on the passenger window of the Toyota. I would then take a photo of the date line with the view of the crutch in the car. Finally, I felt that I had plenty of evidence to defeat any claim she might have made. Jackie told me I made her sleep easier at night by taking these precautions to protect our family's livelihood. Sometimes, we would drink beer and watch the video of this fool playing the doctors.

The couple paid rent on time and were never a problem. They never contacted me to pay any medical bills, either. I think the girl and the children were receiving some kind of assistance, so they didn't need to encroach on our money. But this business relationship came to an end soon on its own accord...

One evening, I received a call from another tenant named David who worked at the hospital. He told me that the police were going to arrest him and that his apartment had been broken into. I didn't understand what the hell was going on, so I drove to the complex.

While David was working at the hospital, his girlfriend, Rita, called the police and said that the Hammericks' son and a friend had tried to break into their apartment. Rita heard them, got a knife, and ran them off. The police were all confused, thinking David was the bad guy. I straightened the policeman out and told him that David was a good renter and that it was his apartment.

I talked to the Hammericks. They apologized and said it would never happen again, but I told them that they had to move out. "Breaking and entering is too serious to get another chance," I said.

The boys informed me that they had just kicked the door in to scare Rita.

I wasn't having any of it. I gave Mr. Hammerick my famous Finished Business speech and let him know he'd get his full deposit back, plus his rent. But only if he could be out of the apartment by Saturday. He got out. And that was the last I saw of him.

In this complex, Jackie and I tried to make it a policy never to rent a two-bedroom apartment to more than two adults. But one day, Jackie got a call from a personnel company needing to rent two apartments for their workers. The company was pulling in Mexican workers for the local flooring plant. Having had such success in dealing with Mexican tenants before, I was fine with it.

These workers turned out to be straight from the rural hill country of Mexico. Jackie met with the personnel manager and some of the prospective tenants and immediately insisted that the personnel manager also sign the lease. Jackie told her that if we had any problems, we would be calling her.

Jackie and I would go to the apartment around the 5th of each month to collect the rent. Someone inside the apartment would always have it.

For the most part, they worked all the time. But when they were off, these guys got *drunk*. Proper drunk. I mean John Wayne movie drunk.

One day, I got a call from the police that there had been a fight in their unit. Upon my arrival, I was surprised to find a trail of blood splattered along the wall of the entrance hall – I guess the police were right. I didn't see anyone hurt, but to my further surprise, I also didn't recognize any of the Mexicans living there. So I knew something was fishy.

Soon after, I discovered that the drunken Mexicans had skipped out on their lease, as well. Fortunately, my wife had been smart enough to get the personnel manager to co-sign. Jackie called and explained the situation to the manager, but the manager wasn't having any of it. She just passed the buck, saying, "Hang on. Let me give you to my superior."

The superior calmly informed us that they were not liable for the damage to the apartment, or of course, for the rent.

So Jackie politely pointed out that his manager had agreed to co-sign the lease. She even offered to fax a copy to his office. See, Jackie was a champion at this kind of thing. She didn't care if the current tenants paid, but she made it clear she would certainly sue the personnel manager. After all, she was the one who put pen to paper.

Naturally, the superior got nervous when he heard that three-letter word "sue." "What do we need to do to settle this matter?" he asked.

Jackie explained. Then, she quickly typed up a settlement agreement and faxed it to his office. After all was said and done, we received enough cash to renovate the damaged units and get them back on the market.

So here's a nice lesson: When negotiating settlements, always aim high. Once in a while, you might run into someone who will actually pay and take responsibility for the damages done by the irresponsible parties.

But get this: Not only did the personnel manager get the company to pay; she was even nice enough to send her own mother to clean the place up. Even better, she did a fine job of it – no blood stains anywhere.

Alright, on a related note, let's talk about uninvited guests. You'll get those all the time, too, reader.

One day, I dropped in to change the air filter in one unit of our twenty-four unit complex. When I first arrived, the unit seemed empty. But then, upon further inspection, I realized that there were a couple of people in the bedroom in the back. When I walked in, I saw two people. Nude. Lying on a mattress on the floor of the room. I didn't recognize them.

"What are you doing here?" I said.

"Our friends said we could stay here for awhile," they said.

Just as I was about to respond, I noticed a medium-sized housecat in the bed with them. The cat wasn't napping or clawing at the sheets like other cats; *this* cat was violently humping the pillow between them.

Strange. But I shook it off.

"You can stay for a couple of days," I said. "But that cat's got to go!"

As time went on, I had two more meetings with this couple, and every time I was over there, that cat was in their bed, screwing their pillow. It didn't take much for me to conclude that the cat was overly horny and the unknown couple was living there illegally. A few days later, this couple fled with the real renters – they all skipped town; luckily, cat included.

When we first figured that we had the twelve-of-twenty-four complex under control (and boy were we wrong), we decided that it would be okay to move out of Hasselville. Ultimately, we moved to Pensacola, Florida. Our boys would have greater opportunities in Pensacola as they prepared to enter high school, we knew. Jackie and I had no problem leaving Hasselville since we had started hiring out most of the work, anyway.

But just before we left for Pensacola, Jackie rented a newly renovated apartment to a guy named Taco. Taco, as you can imagine, was Mexican. He also happened to have a supervisory position at one of the local meat-packing plants. The apartment we rented to him was beautiful. It had wall-to-wall tile and modern everything; you couldn't ask for a better place. But, as one might expect with such a great place, the brand new water heater started leaking right after Taco moved in. Being miles away from Hasselville, I had to call my guys to have it replaced.

Another lesson: No matter how new an appliance is, that doesn't mean it won't break.

The repair guys installed a new water heating unit that day, but they hurried the process. They used a plastic coupling to reconnect the waterline. The next day, while the tenant was at work, the coupling slipped loose and Taco's beautiful, brand new apartment became Taco's Lake Mistake. Even the neighbor called and said water was seeping into his kitchen.

Frustrated, I called my guys back and told them to get their asses over there to assess the damage. A few hours later, they filled me in on what had happened.

"Never use plastic compression coupling inside a house," I said. "Especially near a water heater. You understand?"

I got a roaring affirmative response on that one. A big roger-that.

But that wasn't even the half of it, reader. We'd fixed the issue from an apartment standpoint, sure, but we still hadn't fixed it from a tenant standpoint. And that brings us to another lesson: Tenants will use any disaster as a funnel through which to get free shit.

Pursuant to this lesson, Taco called back and said that his "brand new" computer, a jumper cable machine, a work manual, and a top-of-the-line stereo had been destroyed by the flood. My maintenance guys said that a few things in the closet had gotten wet, as well.

Jackie assured Taco that we would take care of everything. Before we left for Pensacola, she called to let him know that we'd be up after the weekend to look at the damage. He didn't answer the call.

The following Monday, we traveled from Pensacola to Hasselville to check out Taco's apartment.

Headache #1: My guys had fixed the leak, but had used the same plastic coupling I had specifically told them not to use. Naturally, I was furious. I told them to meet me at the apartment. Once they were there, I let them know how much their stupidity was going to cost me. I told them that Taco wanted $1,500 dollars for damages to his property and that the new flooring was swollen and would no doubt need to be replaced too.

Taking a break from chewing them out, I asked them to show me the stuff that had been damaged. My guys lugged it all out onto the living room floor.

Headache #2: I tested the jumper cable machine. It worked. I plugged in the stereo. It worked. I flipped through the work manual. It appeared to be just a copy of what had probably been an expensive original. I found the computer monitor downstairs and the processor upstairs in the closet. I hooked it up and plugged it in. Nothing happened. But then I opened it up to discover that the inside hadn't gotten wet.

So Taco simply needed a new hard drive, but he was trying to rip us off for $1,500.

My first step was to replace the plastic coupling with a metal one. Then, we went back to Pensacola and waited for Taco's call. Eventually, he called Jackie back, wanting to know why we had been in his apartment.

"We drove up from Pensacola to inspect the damage," she said. "We called before we left, but there was no answer."

He was mad as hell. Probably because he knew we were on to his little scam. Anyway, he hung up before my wife could get another word in edgewise.

Glory. This meant another trip back to Hasselville to confront Taco.

I knocked on the door, and when he opened it, Jackie said, "We're here to collect the rent."

"You owe me for damages," Taco said.

"We'll settle damages at a later date," I said. "You signed an agreement to pay the rent on time. If you don't pay the rent, you'll be evicted."

Just like over the phone, he was pissed.

"Again," I said, "we will pay you for the damages, but this is not an opportunity for you to stick us. I looked at all the things you said were broken and they all work just fine."

"I want $350 for the manual."

"Look, it's a company manual," I said. "Bring me a receipt and I'll pay you. For all I know, you just made a copy. And your computer monitor works, but you're missing the hard drive. Give me the hard drive and I'll cover the cost to fix it, too."

"I threw it away," he said.

Before he could get in another word, his wife started yelling at him in Spanish, and then he started yelling back.

By the end of it, he produced a receipt for the manual and said, "Forget it," as if *I* was the one ripping *him* off.

Still, Jackie played the role of the honest businessperson and wrote Taco a check for $500 to cover the cost of the manual and hard drive. She waited for him to write a rent check and then they exchanged checks.

We thought things were settled. Taco was definitely a crook because he moved out the following weekend owing us several thousands of dollars for the remaining time on the lease.

Alright, reader. I don't mean to suggest that we inherited an entire building of assholes. In fact, we were fortunate enough to have quite a few great tenants. Enjoying our new home in Pensacola, Jackie and I talked one night about some of our best tenants. We came to the conclusion that not everyone was bad – they just had the misfortune of having terrible family members.

And you know what? Sometimes you have to stick your neck out in defense of those good tenants if you want them to stick around.

One evening, just about dinnertime, our tenant Nancy called about her door not closing properly because the trim had fallen off. We gladly offered to fix it because Nancy had been a near-perfect renter for quite a few years.

But when I went to her apartment, I noticed that her mother's BMW was parked behind the building. I shrugged. Her mother was an arrogant woman who often complained about the condition of the apartment. *Nancy must take after her father*, I reasoned.

Before we get down to brass tacks, let's have another lesson: Sometimes, you have to have the guts to tell those arrogant or untrustworthy family members to get lost. They're not the ones renting from you, anyway.

I was always patient with the mother. "I have a much better apartment at the 20-unit complex," I would say, "but the rent is about $100 more a month."

"Well," she would say, "my daughter can't afford that...so why don't you make these apartments nicer?"

Typical.

That day, I let her have it in front of her daughter and son-in-law. "Let me tell you something," I said. "You might fool your daughter and son-in-law into thinking you're some high-class rich broad, but I know exactly who and what you are."

She stood speechless, so I let her rip.

"If you don't like your daughter living here, why don't you help her pay for a more expensive apartment? Why not? Because you clearly don't have any money. You're always hiding your shitty BMW from the repo man and you force your complaining self into this tiny apartment with your daughter and her husband when there's a hotel just up the road."

Was I a little harsh? Oh, hell yes. But it worked. That spoiled little stain got up and stormed out like her world had just caved in.

A few days later, I saw the son-in-law at the grocery store (I'd stopped in on my way back to Pensacola to pick up a few things for dinner that night). To my surprise, he shook my hand and said, "I am so glad you told that crazy bitch off. I've wanted to tell her that for years."

Later, I ran into Nancy...and she thanked me, too! Apparently her mother had moved out.

"We're just glad the bitch is gone," she said.

So I let the lady have it and got praised for it. Conversely, no good deed goes unpunished...

At twelve-of-twenty-four, we had a retired soldier as a tenant. He was very polite and lived alone. We saw him fishing at the park just about every Sunday afternoon. His unit definitely needed work, even from the day we bought it, but he had lived there for over ten years and seemed to be content.

But every once in a while, he would call to ask us about getting new flooring throughout. I told him that it would be nearly impossible to get flooring with all his furniture, but I offered him a newly renovated apartment at the same complex for about $95 more per month. I also took him to look at a one-bedroom apartment with new flooring and appliances. He loved the one-bedroom because it didn't have stairs, so I told him he could move into it and pay the same rent he was used to paying. Naturally, he was excited. And Jackie and I were happy for him.

But a few days later, he called and said his kids were fixing a house in Chicago and that they wanted him to move back there when it was finished. So on the one hand, I was disappointed because instead of helping a tenant, I would be losing one. But then the old man never moved.

This would happen once every year, this unfulfilled promise of a new house. I felt bad for the old man because, every year, he would get his hopes up, and every year, the work on his dream house near his kids would never get finished. He was still alone in that apartment the day we sold it.

When the telephone rings, Jackie and I can't be sure what kind of challenge we might face. When it's not a maintenance call, it's a crisis of some sort. One day, Jackie got a call from Judy Lynn. She was in the hospital because her boyfriend beat her up – and she wanted Jackie to come down to the hospital to collect her rent.

Judy Lynn was a tough old woman who rented a two-bedroom apartment from us. She was in her late 60s, but wore the snappy clothes of the 70s – all sharp-looking in her bell-bottom slacks, fro, and leather coat. When I say fro, I mean "messy old woman perm." Nonetheless, she could have been a member of the mod squad. She was such a sweet and fun lady. We both hated to hear about all her troubles.

Judy paid her rent pretty much on time, and if there was ever a problem with it, she always called and got caught up. Our business relationship got so tight that she even called Jackie one day in the middle of the month and asked if she could borrow money. Jackie told her we couldn't do that. We laughed about it, but you can't fault her for trying!

But here's the trouble, reader: it turned out that the guy who was always beating her up had been living with her. Without our knowledge. She asked Jackie to sign a trespass warning on the guy and she agreed. Jackie also gave her the number of the domestic violence shelter where she could receive help and develop a safety plan. But within four weeks of getting home from the hospital, the guy who beat her up was back living with her again. A landlord can only do so much, I guess.

One time, we rented an apartment to an officer in the coast guard. He was the unluckiest guy we ever dealt with. He had unwillingly been involved in the skin-head fight I wrote about earlier. It wasn't just the fights, though. For this guy, the drama never quit.

He called once and said he needed to talk. I could tell it wasn't about the rent, so I drove to the complex to meet with him. Once I arrived, he told me his roommate was being handed a court martial. "My roommate is having an affair with my fiancé while I'm on duty," he said.

"Why are you mad at him?" I asked. "She's obviously a whore. Plus, your roommate's saved you a lot of money just by living here."

He looked stunned and I could tell he didn't like me calling his fiancé a whore. But I could also tell that he knew I was right.

"What did you expect when you moved her into your bachelor pad?" I asked.

By the time I left, the coast guard seemed to be feeling a little better about the situation. He told me that he decided to stop the court martial on his roommate. They soon reconciled.

So these final four stories bring us to the ultimate lesson of this book, reader. Sometimes, if you want to keep your good tenants happy – and I mean the truly good ones, here – you have to go above and beyond the usual duties of a landlord. You have to bend over backward to accommodate their needs, tell off their overbearing relatives, help them find the help they so sorely need, and even serve as a shoulder to cry on once in a while.

In this business, you'll make your friends as well as your enemies. Try not to let the enemies get to you. And always keep your friends close. Do that, and you'll find success even where that sort of thing seems impossible.

Conclusion

It's ironic that I'm sitting in unit 2008 at the Carriage Hills Apartments in my underwear, writing this book. Why is it ironic? Because this is the same unit that Jackie and I lived in when we first moved to Hasselville (with hardly enough money to afford much more than underwear). It's 2am again, but I'm not up because I'm nervous about a sale or frustrated with a tenant; I'm up just because I can be.

I'm back here now because I'm preparing to convert this apartment complex into condominiums– the kind of job everyone in the business hopes for. This transition will be a very lucrative move for our business. Jackie has always dreamed of being able to provide affordable homes for people especially in one of the poorest states in the country. Words can't express how it makes me feel to watch my wife smile as we accomplish the list of her dreams. AMAZING.

I have a wonderful life. Near perfect. God, I sound just like one of those people on the early morning infomercials. Like them, I'm grinning from ear to ear – only I'm not sipping iced tea and soaking in the warm, Hawaiian rays. I'm in my apartment in Hasselville and sitting on a successful business, which suits me just fine.

So, was business all sunshine and roses and smiling faces everywhere, or was it simply hell?

Well, I'll let you decide.

Today, I work a couple of hours a week tending to my property and I live on the beautiful Emerald Coast without much worry. I wake up each morning with a calm sense about me. I won't lie; this is a direct reflection of the wealth I've accumulated (and my healthy sense of pride).

So I now know the *No Money Down* system works. I'm living proof (there I go again). In my opinion, it's the safest, surest way to achieve financial independence, which is the freedom that we all seek. I don't mean the illusion that most people live, I mean *real* financial freedom. The kind of freedom that lets you own your dreams and the kind of wealth that produces, well, more wealth.

I hope that you now have a truer idea of what is involved with the business of real estate. You can't go into it thinking it's going to be smooth sailing or that you'll make your money quick. You also can't jump in too quickly, nor can you be too timid. I went from being a Geology major working with waste – and lacking any iota of self-confidence – to a real-estate entrepreneur with more properties and equity than I knew what to do with. This was not a result of passivity, but of tenacity. It's a lot of hard work, reader.

As made apparent in the stories presented in this book, perhaps the hardest part is the people you'll encounter. You'll certainly meet swindlers, child molesters, and drug addicts – and police officers, as a result. You'll meet complainers, mama's boys, abusers and penny-pinchers. But you'll also meet what I call "Angels." People that inspire you, people that make all the trouble-makers and the disappointment quickly evaporate. That – coupled with the chance to spend every day alongside my business partner/lovely wife – truly made it all worth it.

I suppose I should slow up a bit. Of all my regrets in life, I have one with this business: I wish I could have done in five years what took me fifteen. I'll probably write another book called *The Mistakes I Made,* which might shine more light on the hardships of this business and help others learn from my pitfalls. Might make for a decent book...

So, from my apartment I look back at my life as a *No Money Down* entrepreneur. I look back at the crooks, the angels, and the disappointment. As I sit here, cross-legged, I have to laugh at the crooks, smile at the angels, and move on from the disappointment. As I said, *No Money Down* works, but you quickly learn that while it's not all sunshine and roses, it's certainly not all hell either. It's somewhere in between. And Jackie and I are perfectly happy with that.

www.ingramcontent.com/pod-product-compliance
Lightning Source LLC
Chambersburg PA
CBHW022051210326
41519CB00054B/301